FACTS AT YOUR FINGERTIPS

ENDANGERED ANIMALS

INVERTEBRATES

BROWN
BEAR
BOOKS

Published by Brown Bear Books Limited

4877 N. Circulo Bujia
Tucson, AZ 85718
USA

and

First Floor
9-17 St. Albans Place
London N1 ONX
UK

Library of Congress Cataloging-in-Publication Data

Invertebrates / edited by Tim Harris.
 p. cm. – (Facts at your fingertips. Endangered animals)
 Includes bibliographical references and index.
 Summary: "Describes various invertebrates that are endangered
and at risk of becoming extinct. Data Sheet sidebars and maps
accompany the text"–Provided by publisher.
 ISBN 978-1-936333-33-2 (library binding)
 1. Rare invertebrates–Juvenile literature. 2. Endangered species–
Juvenile literature. I. Harris, Tim. II. Title.

 QL362.45.I68 2012
 592.168–dc22

                                    2010053967

ISBN-13 978-1-936333-33-2

Editorial Director: Lindsey Lowe
Editor: Tim Harris
Creative Director: Jeni Child
Designer: Lynne Lennon
Children's Publisher: Anne O'Daly
Production Director: Alastair Gourlay

Printed in the United States of America

In this book you will see the following key at top left of
each entry. The key shows the level of threat faced by each
animal, as judged by the International Union for the
Conservation of Nature (IUCN).

EX	Extinct
EW	Extinct in the Wild
CR	Critically Endangered
EN	Endangered
VU	Vulnerable
NT	Near Threatened
LC	Least Concern
O	Other (this includes Data Deficient and Not Evaluated)

For a few animals that have not been evaluated since 2001,
the old status of Lower Risk still applies and this is shown by
the letters **LR** on the key.

For more information on Categories of Threat, see pp. 54–57.

Picture Credits

Abbreviations: c=center; t=top; l=left; r=right.

Cover Images
Front: *Birdwing butterfly,* Shutterstock
Back: *Sea-urchin,* Thinkstock/istockphoto

AL: Edwin Mickleburgh 61; **BCC:** 54–55, Jane Bunton 43, Alain
Compost 33 inset, D. W. Frith 33r, Rod Williams 21; **FLPA:** Frants
Hartmann 57, Roger Tidman 7; **IUCN:** 59; **Mark Hutchinson:** 11;
William P. Mull: 23l; **Photolibrary Group:** Animals Animals
44–45, 'J.S' l. Vookr 15, Marty Cordano 56, Tui De Roy 48,
Fredrick Ehrenstrom 13, David Fleetham 41, David Fox 52–43, C.
Lockwood 49, R. L. Manuel 8–9, OSF 27, Norbert Rosing 50-51,
Alastair Shay 4t, E. & J. Woolmer 35; **Photoshot:** Roger Tidman
25, Norbert Wu 6; **PW:** K. G. Preston-Mafham 17; **Robin Crump:**
47; **Dennis R. Seaward:** 51; **Still Pictures:** Hans Pfleschinger
23r; **Thinkstock:** istockphoto 1

Artwork © Brown Bear Books Ltd

*Brown Bear Books has made every attempt to contact the copyright
holder. If you have any information please email
smortimer@brownbearbooks.co.uk*

CONTENTS

What is an Invertebrate?

Invertebrates are animals without backbones. While vertebrates have the same basic plan, with a skull, a jointed backbone extending into the tail, and paired fore- and hind limbs supported by bony girdles, invertebrates have none of these things. There are about 29 major groups of invertebrates that are all very different from the vertebrates and all quite different from each other. Together they make up about 97 percent of the animal kingdom. (The remaining 3 percent of animals are the vertebrates—fish, birds, mammals, and so on.)

Familiar invertebrates include snails, clams, earthworms, flies, wasps, spiders, and starfish; but there are many others, some of which are relatively obscure, such as parasitic flukes and tapeworms.

Invertebrates play a large part in human health. Some are responsible for transmitting diseases such as malaria that afflict hundreds of millions of people. Although modern medicine has done much to reduce their effects, malaria is once again a very serious problem in some parts of the world from which it had once been eliminated.

Invertebrates such as locusts, aphids, slugs, and wireworms are crop pests. Termites and wood-boring beetles can cause major structural problems in timber houses and destroy timber and paper products. Clearly some invertebrates exert considerable pressures on humans, while others are useful to people. For example, ants and earthworms do much to improve the quality of soils by burrowing and turning over the soil particles. Bees produce honey, while oysters and crayfish are eaten around the world. Some invertebrates are the source of useful drugs and medicinal products, for example, the anticoagulants of leeches or the antiarthritis drugs taken from green mussels. Others, like many butterfly species, are simply very beautiful to look at. Insects are invertebrates, and without them it would have been necessary for plant life to have evolved different methods of pollination.

Invertebrate Diversity

There is an astonishing range of invertebrate structures and lifestyles. Adult sea-urchins, for example, are round and heavy with chalky skeletons. They have no head, they defend their bodies with spines and minute, forceplike grooming organs, and they move around on the seabed with hydraulic limbs. Inside the mouth are five well-developed teeth that scrape plants off the rocks on which they live. Their eggs develop into microscopic larvae that drift at the surface of the sea. These larvae are unlike their parents in appearance and lifestyle. They are not round or heavy, and they have a right and left side. But they turn into juvenile sea-urchins and sink to the bottom of the sea.

Compare the sea-urchin with a soft-bodied flatworm living amid the vegetation at the bottom of a pond. Here is an animal that has a head with rudimentary eyes and smelling organs; it has a mouth but no anus, and its soft body ends in a tail. The flatworm glides over the pond floor, feeding on rotting vegetation and bacteria. Its body is light and needs no hard skeleton for the muscles to pull on. These two examples give us a glimpse of the range of animal architecture among invertebrates. Compare them with the honey bee, a flying insect that can communicate, harvest pollen, live socially, and make honey. The range of invertebrate forms and activity is huge.

Defining Characteristics

Scientists have established a number of fundamental characteristics that help establish the classification and

Mollusks *share common structural features. The phylum Mollusca includes sea hares (1), giant clams (2), octopuses (3), chetoderms (4), chitons (5), razor shells (6), elephant's tusk shells (7), dog whelks (8), European whelks (9), and Neopilina, limpetlike mollusks (10).*

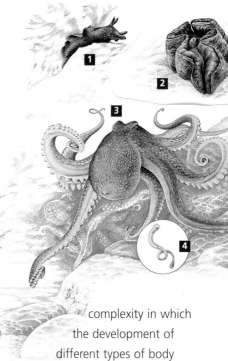

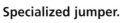

Specialized jumper.
The desert locust (above) is an arthropod with a jointed exoskeleton.

evolutionary relationships of invertebrates. They include features such as symmetry. Some animals, such as sponges, are asymmetrical (having no particular shape). Some, such as sea anemones and corals, are radially symmetrical (having no head and with the mouth in the middle of a circular, saclike body). Some, like worms and insects, are bilaterally symmetrical (having a head and with the body developed into left and right sides). Other distinguishing characteristics include whether the cells of the body are organized into tissues and how many tissue layers make up the body. The presence or absence and type of cavity inside the body are also considered important. All these distinctions are rather technical. But the result is that the invertebrates can be arranged in an order of increasing evolutionary complexity in which the development of different types of body architecture can be understood and the relationships between phyla can be predicted.

The History of Invertebrates

Although we believe that the first primitive land vertebrates appeared over 275 million years ago during the Carboniferous period, the fossil record tells us that the invertebrates have been in existence for much longer, probably about 650 million years. We depend on the existence of fossils that can be dated in order to determine the longevity of animal groups. Nowadays special techniques enable us to determine the age of fossils with considerable accuracy.

The Paleozoic era stretched from 650 million years ago to 225 million years ago, and it is divided into seven periods. The earliest, the Ediacarian (650 to 570 million years ago) saw the appearance of the first animal fossils. They are not easily assigned to any phyla we know today, but resembled present-day sea anemones, worms, and jointed limbed creatures.

By the end of the next period, the Cambrian (570 to 500 million years ago), invertebrates with hard skeletons had begun to appear. They fossilized quite well, and most of the phyla we recognize today were represented, including trilobites (a kind of crustacean), brachiopods (a type of mollusk), and primitive echinoderms (sea-urchins). By the end of the Ordovocian period (500 to 430 million years ago) most of the classes of invertebrates we recognize today had established themselves, and some, such as the echinoderms and nautiloid mollusks, had reached their peak of development. The shorter Silurian period (430 to 395 million years ago) saw the decline of some of the great marine groups, but terrestrial invertebrates such as millipedes began to appear on land. Arachnids and wingless insects next appeared on land in the Devonian period, and winged insects developed in

Anchor damage *by small boats visiting coral reefs is just one example of thoughtless harm to the environment.*

the Carboniferous period that ended 280 million years ago. At this time there was a slow decline in the diversification of life forms, and by the end of the Permian period (225 million years ago) most groups had dramatically declined; in fact, many had become extinct, probably as a result of the cooling of the earth.

A slow recovery in invertebrate diversity began. During the Jurassic period (192 to 135 million years ago) most of the modern orders of animals became established, and invertebrate classification would have started to look much the same as it does today. Development declined in the Cretaceous period. Coming to the

An Arctic seabed community
during the Cretaceous period (135 to 64 million years ago). Organisms included the belemnite (1), ammonite (2), sea anemone (3), gastropod (4), sea-urchin (5), bivalve mollusk (6), and crab (7).

Tertiary period—beginning 64 million years ago—most genera and families of invertebrates were established.

Why are Invertebrates at Risk?

Many invertebrates are small, and some lack sophisticated means of controlling what is inside them. Some—the marine forms—therefore take on an internal environment and salt and water balance that resembles seawater itself. Others that live in fresh water may have only the crudest mechanisms to control their osmotic balance (how much water and salt they have in their bodies), and quite a few simple terrestrial forms cannot survive out of contact with moist soils. Thus in many cases such species are unable to prevent their bodies taking in chemical pollutants or are unable to control the loss of moisture if the environment becomes starved of water. For those invertebrates that are attached to the sea floor, such as corals and sponges, changes in seawater levels can be disastrous, and changes in temperature cannot be overcome by migratory movements. In contrast, a number of other endangered invertebrate species, such as butterflies and dragonflies, are highly mobile, but their life cycles may demand a particular type of vegetation or aquatic environment for their larvae to develop in. Such environments are frequently damaged or destroyed by human activity, especially the development of industries or urban areas.

The Situation Today

Because invertebrates are relatively unknown and often lack the charisma of the large vertebrates such as mammals, they do not gain the same amount of public support. People are much more likely to contribute to conservation of the panda than an endangered beetle or spider species.

Furthermore, it is difficult to give precise figures on the endangered status of the invertebrates. There are probably over 40,000 species of vertebrate, but no one knows how many species of invertebrate exist on earth. Nearly 1,400,000 have been named, but probably many more exist. Even so, the number of described species is vast, and it is difficult to get data on how many of these invertebrates are under threat. Recent estimates suggest that more than 2,600 are affected, but since this is less than twice the number of recognized threatened mammals, it is almost certainly an underestimation of the real situation.

Statistics can be misleading. From the figures in the table below, in the IUCN Red List 2008, you might think that very few invertebrate species are threatened—just 0.5 percent of the total assessed, in comparison with 27 percent of mammal species. But the number of invertebrate species is huge. And of the species studied, the percentage assessed as threatened is higher than for mammals. Are 35 percent of invertebrates under threat? No. Scientists could not evaluate all insects, as they do mammals, so they look at those species that are rarer and more likely to be under threat.

This display *of butterflies and tarantulas is a sad reminder of the continuing trade in animal specimens.*

Numbers of species *and percentages of mammals and invertebrates threatened in 2008.*

Threatened Mammals and Invertebrates

	No. of species in group	No. of threatened species
Mammals	5,488	1,466
Invertebrates	1,400,000	2,639
	% of total in group threatened	% of total assessed threatened
Mammals	27%	27%
Invertebrates	0.5%	35%

EX

EW

CR

EN

VU

NT

LC

O

Broad Sea Fan

Eunicella verrucosa

The sea fan is a type of coral made up of many simple polyps joined together to form a colony in a fanlike pattern. In common with a number of other marine invertebrates, sea fans are beautiful and often form major attractions in "submarine gardens." A slow-growing animal, it is now under threat from overcollection.

Sea fans are found in most of the world's seas and oceans. They may grow from shallow water down to the edge of the continental shelves and beyond; they are even found at depths of about 13,000 feet (4,000 m) in some parts of the world. The broad sea fan occurs in the northeastern Atlantic and in the Mediterranean Sea. Sea fans are attractive to souvenir hunters, and thoughtless collecting by divers has recently reduced their populations around European coasts.

Sea fans are colonial, that is, they are made up of many individual polyps, or zooids—cylindrical forms joined together to form a colony. Such a lifestyle is not unusual in the phylum Cnidaria to which they belong. In the broad sea fan the polyps are arranged in two rows along the top and bottom of the branches.

Each polyp is a miniature animal in its own right and has its own mouth that also serves as its anus. The mouth is surrounded by eight minute branching tentacles that are armed with stinging cells. The tentacle form is a feature of the order Gorgonacea (horny corals) and is ideal for sieving the passing water currents to trap microscopic plankton. Once collected, the prey is manipulated into the gastric cavity via the mouth. The gastric cavity extends into a number of tubes that increase the surface area for absorption and digestion of food products. Many species of sea fan are virtually two dimensional, and they grow so that the colony faces the prevailing currents at right angles, thus maximizing their ability to catch prey. Growth is slow, so some sea fans are very old.

The colony is supported by an internal horny skeleton made up of a substance called gorgonin. The tissue from which the polyps are made is further supported and protected by crystals of calcium carbonate that are embedded within it.

DATA PANEL

Broad sea fan

Eunicella verrucosa

Family: Anthozoa

World population: Unknown

Distribution: Mediterranean Sea; northeastern Atlantic; off coasts of France, Ireland, U.K., Mauritania, Morocco, Portugal, and Spain

Habitat: Rocks and hard surfaces from 49 ft (15 m) downward to about 984 ft (300 m)

Size: Colony grows to 11.8 in (30 cm) in height

Form: Plantlike pink or white colony made up of polyps—cylindrical sessile (attached) forms; branches in 1 plane only. Individual polyps arranged in double rows

Diet: Minute drifting plankton

Breeding: Details not well known; planula (free-swimming larva) results from fertilization of eggs; attaches itself to a new substrate; develops into a new colony, which produces new zooids

Related endangered species: Probably many, including red coral (*Corallium rubrum*)

Status: IUCN VU

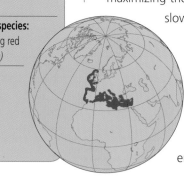

Sperms and eggs develop inside the polyps, and fertilization results in the development of a planula (free-swimming larva), which escapes from the "parent" via its mouth and swims into the sea. The planula has a simple structure and is covered with microscopic beating filaments (cilia) that drive it through the water. However, the planula can detect a suitable substratum—usually rock—on which to settle and develop into a new colony, producing at first a founder polyp. The polyp grows and produces more individual polyps and the necessary skeleton so that a colony structure is developed once again.

Vulnerability

The emerging interest in marine conservation has led to an increased awareness of the effects of overcollection and human disturbance on some marine animals and plants. Although it has not been significantly at risk in the past, threats to the broad

Sea fans come in a variety of colors, from deep red, yellow, and orange to pink and white. The polyps spread out their tentacles, forming a net with which they catch plankton.

sea fan have risen recently with the increase in popularity of scuba diving. The broad sea fan and its Mediterranean relative, red coral (*Corallium rubrum*), are both slow growing, so they are potentially more vulnerable. Unlike the broad sea fan, *Corallium* has been collected for centuries, certainly since classical times. A rich red color, it was considered semiprecious and made into jewelry by the Greeks and Romans; it was also thought to be able to ward off illnesses. *Corallium* is now scarce in the Mediterranean and is found only at great depths. Collection of the animal seems as yet to be poorly regulated.

Giant Gippsland Earthworm

Megascolides australis

One of the largest earthworms in the world, the giant Gippsland earthworm was discovered in 1878. Its large size and secretive habits have made it vulnerable to changes in land use resulting from the development of agricultural land from natural forest.

The giant Gippsland earthworm belongs to the Phylum Annelida, the segmented worms, which includes earthworms, ragworms, and leeches. Named after the area of Australia that is its home, it is found only in Gippsland, a fertile region of southeastern Victoria that extends along the coast from Melbourne to the New South Wales border.

The giant Gippsland earthworm lives in permanent and elaborate burrows, spending all its life underground. There it feeds on the roots of plants and on other organic matter in the soil. Most earthworm species deposit their waste material as obvious casts on the surface, but this species leaves its cast material below ground.

As a result of its exclusively underground life the giant Gippsland earthworm is difficult to study. Consequently, many aspects of its biology are unknown. We do know that its body is divided up into between 300 to 500 visible segments. The head and front third of the body are a dark purple color, while the remainder, behind the "saddle," is a pinkish-gray.

Giant Gippsland earthworms are not easily kept in captivity, and because of their large size and fragility they are easily damaged or killed by scientists and farmers alike.

Patchy Distribution

The distribution of the giant Gippsland earthworm was previously much wider than it is today. When European settlers arrived in the 18th century, they transformed large areas of native forest into pasture for the dairy industry. The disturbances associated with this proved very damaging to the worms.

Today giant Gippsland earthworms tend to be restricted to steep hillsides and valleys where the soils cannot be plowed. Any activities that affect the moisture content and drainage of the soil can also be bad news for the worms. Building roads and dams,

DATA PANEL

Giant Gippsland earthworm

Megascolides australis

Family: Megascolecidae

World population: Unknown

Distribution: Restricted to about 40 square miles (100 sq. km) of land in Gippsland, Victoria, Australia

Habitat: Burrows in organically rich soils

Size: Length: 31 in (80 cm); diameter 0.8 in (2 cm)

Form: Typical segmented worm; a definite head and 300–500 segments each with chaetae (bristles); well-developed respiratory and vascular system

Diet: Plant tissue and organic matter in soil

Breeding: Worms are hermaphrodite, but 2 individuals are required for fertilization to occur. Mating takes place in spring and early summer.

Individuals lay a single amber-colored egg capsule containing 1 embryo, which takes about 12 months to hatch. The earthworms are presumed to reach adulthood about 4.5 years after hatching. Adults may be long-lived

Related endangered species: Washington giant earthworm (*Driloleirus americanus*) VU; Oregon giant earthworm (*D. macelfreshi*) VU

Status: IUCN VU

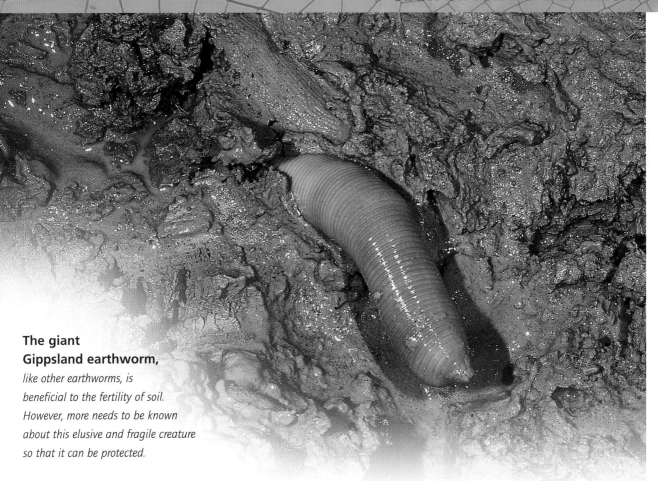

The giant Gippsland earthworm, *like other earthworms, is beneficial to the fertility of soil. However, more needs to be known about this elusive and fragile creature so that it can be protected.*

trenching, and laying cables are all damaging activities. Natural seasonal fluctuations of moisture content govern the normal movement of the worms within the soil.

Recent surveys of southern and western Gippsland have shown that the giant earthworm is restricted to about 40 square miles (100 sq. km) of land in an area bounded approximately by Loch, Korumburra, and Warragul. Much of this land is unsuitable, and the giant earthworm's distribution is very patchy. The population density of the adult worms within the acceptable areas is usually low, about two individuals per 35 cubic feet (two per cubic meter). The worms are mostly found in blue-gray clay soils on flats by the banks of streams or along ditches and watercourses where the slopes face a southwesterly direction.

Like all earthworms, the giant Gippsland worms have beneficial effects on the quality of the soil in which they live, contributing to an increase in its organic content and assisting aeration and increasing fertility. The giant Gippsland earthworm has become part of the folklore of southern Gippsland, and many landowners speak with pride about its presence on their properties.

Conservation

Conserving the giant Gippsland earthworm is difficult. Retaining natural vegetation alongside streams as well as on steep slopes and in valleys and keeping out livestock by fencing the remaining earthworm habitats are both thought to be helpful measures. However, such strategies rely heavily on the cooperation of private landowners and farmers who may need help in identifying the parts of their properties that accommodate the giant earthworms. One issue that has recently made this more difficult is the splitting up of larger properties into smaller ones used for small-scale farming.

Edible Sea-Urchin

Echinus esculentus

Sadly, the beautifully colored edible sea-urchin has become a familiar sight in beach souvenir shops. The animal is collected extensively because its test (shell-like internal skeleton) makes popular decorative objects and souvenirs.

Sea-urchins are spiny-skinned invertebrates that are in the same phylum—Echinodermata—as sea lilies, starfish, brittle stars, and sea cucumbers. Like other echinoderms, they have no head and no true brain, and their bodies have a skeleton of chalky plates. There are about 800 species of sea-urchin.

Sea-urchins are important grazers in marine communities. By eating young and developing algae (plants without true stems, roots, and leaves), they play a major role in controlling vegetation growth in the sea. They also feed on encrusting animals such as barnacles and sea mats. A lack of sea-urchins in a given area can result in rapid algal growth, and in some sensitive habitats such as coral reefs this can have serious effects on other organisms; the plants quickly outcompete the slower-growing corals for both light and space.

The edible sea-urchin is a temperate species, living on hard substrates and among larger algae in coastal waters around northwestern Europe. Compared with other species of sea-urchin, it is quite large and has a pale, rosy-pink test. The test is the shell-like internal skeleton that is so close to the outside of the animal that it appears to be a shell. However, it is covered by thin living tissue. The skeleton of sea-urchins, as in other echinoderms, is made up of crystals of calcium carbonate perforated by spaces. (As a result, it is easily occupied by minerals after the animal's death, so it fossilizes well.)

The sea-urchin's test bears whitish-pink needle-shaped spines with purple tips. They are used for defense against predators and as an aid to the animal's movement. Between the spines are the pedicellariae—minute pincerlike organs carried on stalks—that are used for grooming.

As well as spines sea-urchins also have many long, branched tentacles, called tube-feet, with suckers on the end, which are arranged in rows up and down the animals. They are hollow and can be filled with water from inside the animal and extended by hydraulic pressure. They are used for movement and balance, and in some species help act as a sort of camouflage.

Like other sea-urchins, the edible sea-urchin has a mouth on the underside of the test with a complex arrangement of five jaws with teeth that are extruded (thrust out) to scrape

DATA PANEL

Edible sea-urchin

Echinus esculentus

Family: Echinidae

World population: Unknown

Distribution: Northeastern Atlantic

Habitat: Rocks and seaweeds from the low tide mark down to 164 ft (50 m)

Size: Up to 6.7 in (17 cm) diameter; often smaller

Form: Globular body with calcareous test bearing movable spines and extendible tube-feet ending in suckers

Diet: Encrusting animals such as barnacles; large algae

Breeding: Seasonal spawning; fertilization occurs in the open water; free-swimming larva feeds on minute drifting plants until it metamorphoses to form a juvenile urchin

Related endangered species: Probably several, including the rock borer *Paracentrotus lividus* (no common name) not listed by IUCN. The species has been seriously overfished for its edible roe in parts of France and Ireland

Status: IUCN LRnt

algae and other encrusting plant and animal life from the rocks. When removed from the test but still joined together, the jaws resemble a Greek lantern; Aristotle referred to them as lantern teeth, and today the jaw arrangement is called an Aristotle's lantern.

Hunted Out

The edible sea-urchin was for centuries fished for its roe (eggs); the food was considered a delicacy in Tudor times (between 1485 and 1603). Unlike the smaller Mediterranean species *Paracentrotus lividus*, which has a more delicate roe, the relatively coarse roe of the edible sea-urchin is no longer considered desirable to eat.

The edible sea-urchin, *which used to be fished for its edible roe (eggs), is now collected for its beautiful test.*

The species is easily seen and collected under water. When the test is cleaned out by removing the intestine and reproductive organs, it makes an attractive ornament. In recent decades divers have collected edible sea-urchins from southwestern Britain in such large numbers that scientists now believe that a population crash may be imminent. However, further information is needed about the state of the natural populations of edible sea-urchin around northwestern Europe and the sea-urchin's life span so that measures can be taken to protect them.

Velvet Worms

Families Peripatidae and Peripatopsidae

Some scientists have regarded the velvet worms as "missing links" in the evolutionary chain of the animal kingdom. Their habitat—in the litter of the forest floor in moist areas—makes them vulnerable to human activities such as logging and forest clearance.

Velvet worms are terrestrial invertebrates that are placed in their own phylum: Onychophora (meaning claw-bearers). As a result of their widely scattered distribution and nocturnal habits, velvet worms are poorly known; few scientists have had the opportunity to observe live examples. The best known genus in the phylum is *Peripatus*, of which there are about 20 species. Velvet worms look like large caterpillars. They are covered in dry, velvety skin, and they have about 20 pairs of short legs.

Missing Links

Scientists have considered velvet worms as "missing links," lying somewhere in the evolutionary progression between annelids (earthworms and their allies) and arthropods (crustaceans, insects, and spiders). For example, velvet worms have antennae and clawlike mandibles (mouth parts) like arthropods, but their eyes are similar in structure to those of annelids, and they have a thin, flexible body wall (like annelids) rather than an exoskeleton. They move by contracting sheets of muscle (and with little assistance from their soft, unjointed legs), like worms.

Fossil evidence suggests that velvet worms existed 500 million years ago. There are about 70 species of Onychophora in widely separated parts of the world, indicating that the Onychophora are an animal group that evolved before the ancient land masses separated. However, whether velvet worms are forerunners of today's centipedes and millipedes (arthropods) is debatable. Recent research suggests that velvet worms may indeed be closer to modern-day arthropods than annelids and that they should

perhaps be classified as such. In due course the exact classification of velvet worms will be worked out on the basis of molecular investigations.

Slime Attack

The body of the velvet worm is divided into between 14 and 44 segments (depending on the species). Each segment has a pair of short legs with curved claws on the feet. Since they have no skeleton, the worms can squeeze through small holes. They hunt at night, feeding on small insects and cutting up prey with their strong jaws.

On either side of the intestine are glands that produce a sticky slime, which is squirted from a pair of papillae or fingerlike projections on both sides of the mouth. On contact with air the slime solidifies into sticky threads. Small animals readily become entangled in the threads, although the mechanism is thought to be more for defense than to subdue prey.

Moisture Dependent

Velvet worms live in leaf litter on the forest floor, under stones or logs, or in the soil. Their skin has pits that are connected to thin breathing tubes (tracheae). Since there are so many openings and because they cannot be closed, water vapor is constantly lost from the body. (Arthropods have fewer such openings, and theirs can be closed.) In the velvet worm's moist habitat, however, water loss is compensated for: The worms take up water through minute pouches situated near the base of their legs. They fill the pouches by pressing up against damp surfaces. Water is also replaced by drinking the body fluids of insect prey.

Velvet worms are vulnerable to many aspects of human activity. Clearing of the forests by logging, the development of farmland, and the construction of highways all seriously damage the moist forest habitat on which the worms depend. The velvet worms are also at a disadvantage: Unlike many other animals, they cannot move rapidly enough over short periods to redistribute themselves into new habitats.

One of the *Peripatus* species, Macroperipatus insularis *of Jamaica, giving birth.*

DATA PANEL

Velvet worm

***Peripatus* spp. (about 20 species)**

Family: Peripatidae

World population: Unknown

Distribution: West Indies, Central America, and northern regions of South America

Habitat: Southern temperate and tropical forests, among leaf litter and under bark

Size: Length: females up to 5.9 in (15 cm) long; males shorter

Form: Cylindrical body; conspicuous antennae on head; clawlike mandible; thin body wall; 14–43 pairs of short, soft unjointed legs

Diet: Plant material; also insects and other worms

Breeding: Sexes separate; male places capsule of sperm on skin of female. Her white blood cells digest skin under capsule, allowing sperm to enter blood stream; when sperm have found their way to the ovary, they migrate through the ovarian wall and fertilize eggs. Eggs develop and are nourished in uterus. Live young born after a gestation period of about 13 months

Related endangered species: About 70 species of velvet worm; 20 species of the genus *Peripatus*. All are probably vulnerable to destruction of moist forest habitats by logging and development

Status: IUCN EN

UNITED STATES
BAHAMAS
CUBA
Cayman Islands (U.K.)
JAMAICA

Southern Damselfly

Coenagrion mercuriale

Damselflies and their close relatives the dragonflies are familiar waterside insects that hunt their prey on the wing. The drainage of ponds and marshes for agriculture and urban development—as well as an increase in the use of pesticides—threatens to wipe out these beautiful insects.

The brilliantly colored southern damselfly frequents sluggish streams in lowland areas. In Britain it is restricted to a handful of counties such as Hampshire and Dorset in the south of the country. It is more widely distributed across northwestern Europe, from France and Germany southward to the Mediterranean. Southern damselflies are also known to exist in North Africa.

Damselflies and dragonflies are familiar pond and streamside insects. Both have long, slender bodies, keen eyesight, and two pairs of wings. However, it is not difficult to tell the two insects apart. Damselflies are generally smaller and slimmer than their close relatives. In dragonflies the front wings and hind wings are of different shapes, with the hind wings being generally broader. In damselflies the wings are the same shape and taper into a narrow stalk just before they join the body. The two types of insect also alight and rest differently. Dragonflies always rest with their wings outspread, while damselflies perch with their wings only partly spread or held vertically over the body.

The southern damselfly is a day-flying insect, and eyesight is important in all its activities. In many cases the eyes are so large that the head appears to consist of little else. However, damselfly eyes are not quite as dominant as those of the dragonfly and are set farther apart, making the front end of the animal look slightly hammer shaped. Since the head can swivel on the neck, the insects have almost 360-degree vision.

Correspondingly, the senses of smell and touch are less well developed. The jaws are well equipped for biting and strongly toothed, a fact reflected in the name of the order: Odonata, meaning "toothed." The damselfiles are harmless to humans, but feed on a variety of small insects such as mosquitoes and small flies, which they hunt down on the wing.

Reproduction

The reproductive lives of southern damselflies are closely connected with the water by which they live. The long, slender abdomen of the male is equipped with a pair of claspers situated near its rear tip. Just in front of the claspers are the openings of the male reproductive organs. When preparing to mate, the male transfers a drop of sperm from the

---

DATA PANEL

Southern damselfly

Coenagrion mercuriale

Family: Coenagrionidae

World population: Unknown, decreasing

Distribution: Southern Britain; northwestern Europe from France and Germany southward to the Mediterranean; North Africa

Habitat: Slow-running streams and boggy ground

Size: Length: 0.9–1.2 in (2.4–2.7 cm); wingspan: 1–1.4 in (2.5–3.5 cm)

Form: Resembles small dragonfly; long, slim, brilliantly colored body; conspicuous eyes; 2 pairs of wings

Diet: Adults feed on small insects, including mosquitoes; nymphs (larvae) feed on small aquatic animals such as other insect larvae

Breeding: Males go in search of females in spring. After courtship and copulation eggs laid under water in water plants. Free-living larvae hatch and may feed for many weeks before emerging to molt as adult damselflies

Related endangered species: Several, including Frey's damselfly (*Coenagrion hylas freyi*) CR

Status: IUCN NT

opening by bending his abdomen forward and underneath to touch special receptacles near the front of the abdomen (just behind the last pair of walking legs). He then flies off to find a female to mate with and takes hold of her by the neck using his claspers. Mating is then achieved as the male perches holding the female while she bends her abdomen around under his body to touch her tip against his sperm-filled receptacles. She then takes some sperm into her reproductive tract. After mating, the pair may fly around in the "tandem" position, with the male towing the female; this may often be observed in the spring. The female damselfly then dips the tip of her abdomen in the water to touch a suitable water plant. She makes a small cut with her egg-laying appendage and deposits her eggs in the plant tissue.

The eggs hatch into an aquatic larvae known as nymphs. The larvae live in the water and breathe by means of gills carried on three tail projections at the tip of the abdomen. Like adults, the nymphs are carnivores and hunt for aquatic food, small worms, and the larvae of other insects. They have a specially adapted set of mouthparts called the mask. It is normally kept folded under the head, but can be extended with great speed, effectively spearing the victim on the terminal clawlike extensions.

The southern damselfly's *brilliant coloration is due to pigments and the optical properties of the outer layer of the body.*

Conflict over Conservation

Because of its rarity the southern damselfly has recently become the subject of government-sponsored conservation efforts in Britain. Plans are in progress to allow swiftly flowing trout streams and the well-drained land associated with them to deteriorate naturally into habitat that is more suitable for the endangered southern damselfly, namely slower-running waters with boggy ground and soft banks.

The proposals have given rise to conflict between the trout-fishing lobby and conservationists, but this has only served to highlight the needs of the southern damselfly. It is difficult to convince some people of the need to protect the damselfly, but slow progress is being made.

Orange-spotted Emerald

Oxygastra curtisii

The orange-spotted emerald is extinct in Britain as a result of sewage pollution of its last surviving breeding areas. Although it is still found in low densities in some parts of Europe, its populations are vulnerable to the effects of agriculture and other human activities on its aquatic habitat.

The orange-spotted emerald is a dragonfly species that is now extinct in Britain. It was finally extinguished from the British fauna when a sewage leak polluted its last known habitat in southwestern England. However, it remains in low numbers in western and southern Europe and North Africa. In common with its close relative the damselfly, the dragonfly also depends on fresh water for the completion of its life cycle.

Both dragonflies and damselflies have large, paired eyes that are the most conspicuous structures on their heads, and in the dragonflies the eyes are so large that they virtually meet in the midline. Damselfly eyes are not quite as large, but eyesight is important to both groups. Flying dragonflies can apparently detect moving objects at distances of 39 feet (12 m). When hunting, most individuals patrol fixed beats or hunting grounds, pausing to rest with their wings outstretched on favored resting points that are frequently revisited. Damselflies, on the other hand, rest with their wings partly folded. The shape of the wings also helps distinguish between the two types. Dragonflies have hind wings that are broader than the forewings, and both pairs taper only slightly where they meet the body. The fore and hind wings of damselflies are the same size and show a conspicuous taper just before they join the body.

Territorial

Adult dragonflies spend some of their time near water, but may travel for long distances while they are hunting for prey. Their prey takes the form of small insects, especially other flies and mosquitoes that are caught on the wing. Any male that detects another male of the same species trespassing on his beat will engage him in a fight, and broken legs and torn wings are sometimes sustained in such encounters.

Occasionally, dragonflies engage in migrations or travel for long distances. Two species from continental Europe have been recorded venturing over the sea into southern Britain. However, salt water is not liked by dragonflies for breeding purposes, and only a few species can tolerate brackish (slightly salty) water. Males usually mate with females of the same species that enter their territory, and the mating and egg-laying process is similar to that shown

DATA PANEL

Orange-spotted emerald

Oxygastra curtisii

Family: Corduliidae

World population: Unknown, stable

Distribution: Northwestern and central Europe

Habitat: Rivers, streams, and ponds

Size: Length: about 1.7 in (4.5 cm); wingspan: 2.6 in (6.5 cm)

Form: Adult: typical dragonfly head with conspicuous eyes; long body with 2 pairs of wings, hind wings broader than forewings. Larva: wingless aquatic insect; head with retractile jaws; tail lacks external gill filaments

Diet: Adults feed on small insects, including mosquitoes. Nymphs (larvae) feed on small aquatic animals such as other insect larvae

Breeding: Male looks for females in spring. After courtship and copulation eggs are laid underwater in water plants. Free-living larvae hatch and may feed for many weeks before emerging to molt as adult dragonflies

Related endangered species: Ohio emerald dragonfly (*Somatochlora hineana*) NT; banded bog-skimmer dragonfly (*Williamsonia lintneri*) VU; Calvert's emerald (*S. calverti*) NT

Status: IUCN NT

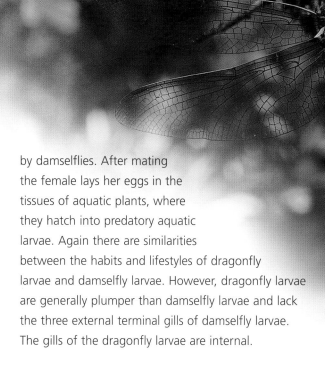

by damselflies. After mating the female lays her eggs in the tissues of aquatic plants, where they hatch into predatory aquatic larvae. Again there are similarities between the habits and lifestyles of dragonfly larvae and damselfly larvae. However, dragonfly larvae are generally plumper than damselfly larvae and lack the three external terminal gills of damselfly larvae. The gills of the dragonfly larvae are internal.

Adult orange-spotted emeralds *hunt in woodlands, around lakes, and along riverbanks. They take their insect prey—including mosquitoes and other flies—on the wing.*

Halting the Decline

It is ironic that despite increasing environmental awareness, current pressures from agriculture, building, and infrastructure development continue to exclude established species from their typical habitats: It is the dragonflies' need for specific conditions for reproduction that makes them vulnerable to any kind of disturbance to their aquatic habitat. However, while humans are largely responsible for the decline in orange-spotted dragonfly numbers, there is also much that can be done to help protect the species. For example, restoring water bodies, digging ponds, and preventing plant overgrowth are some of the steps that can be taken to preserve the quality of aquatic habitats. It is also vital that the consequences of

sewage and industrial pollution are clearly understood and that recreational sources of pollution, from boats and vacation homes, for example, are prevented.

One of the difficulties facing conservationists is that different dragonfly species have different freshwater requirements. Some like running water, while others prefer still water or wetlands, including bogs. The effects of development and its associated drainage of such habitats are different in every case.

Dragonflies have been frequenting water bodies since the Carboniferous period 300 million years ago. About 210 million years ago, in the Jurassic period, there were dragonflies similar to those of today. It is unthinkable that future generations should not see dragonflies like the orange-spotted emerald.

Red-kneed Tarantula

Euathlus smithi

Although there are many species of tarantula, the different forms generally share similar characteristics. Their large, hairy bodies are often strikingly marked, and some species have become popular as pets. Collection of the red-kneed tarantula has put the wild population at risk.

The red-kneed tarantula is arguably the most popular of all pet tarantulas, and people have been collecting specimens since the 1970s. First discovered in 1888, the spider was soon recognized as having potential as a pet. It was also used to heighten tension in films such as *Raiders of the Lost Ark*. Such publicity encouraged collection, and tarantulas were sold in pet stores for many years.

The red-kneed tarantula is found mainly in Mexico and Central America. Its natural habitat is scrubland and desert that provide temperatures of 70–90°F (20–30°C) and humidity of about 60 percent. The spider is found near cacti and bushes, and among logs, rocks, and other debris. It digs burrows in the ground that it lines with spider silk.

For most of the time the spider is relatively docile. However, a threatened red-kneed tarantula will rear up and display the red bristles on its body. As a defensive measure it will flick off urticating (irritant) hairs in the direction of its predator. The hairs are microscopically barbed (having tiny hooks) and can be irritating to the skin and lungs, causing a form of urticaria (an allergic disorder). Serious damage can occur if any hairs become embedded in the eye. Although most people are not seriously affected by the spider's venom, some are allergic to it and can have a strong adverse reaction.

Intriguing Habits

The red-kneed tarantula has a typical spider form, including a pair of fangs (chelicerae) that it uses to stab prey and inject venom. Pedipalps—small appendages near the mouth—have a number of functions, including handling prey. The spiders have poor vision, but sensory structures on the end of the legs allow them to smell, taste, and feel.

The tarantula does not spin a web to catch its food; insects, small amphibians, and sometimes mice are actively hunted at night. The prey is subdued with venom and then flooded with digestive juices. Tarantulas are unable to digest food internally, so the digested "soup" of nutritionally valuable parts of the prey are sucked back by the spider.

Males are often eaten by their mates after mating. When mature, a male spider spins a tubular web in which he deposits sperm. He then draws the sperm up into a special receptacle in his pedipalps. When mating is about to start, the male makes courtship signals, which help ensure that the female does not mistake him for prey. He uses tibial spurs (sharp projections) to grip the female's fangs while placing sperm in the female's reproductive tract.

Black Market

Although red-kneed tarantulas are relatively easy to keep, they are not easy to breed in captivity. The females live for a long time, often up to 20 years in captivity, but their reproductive rate tends to be slow. As a result of their popularity with collectors and the tarantula's vulnerability to habitat change, the species has become seriously threatened. Populations could not sustain the demands of the pet trade, and the wild spiders are now difficult to find. Mexico has prohibited their capture and export, but a black market still exists: Smugglers have been caught trying to take them out of their native countries.

DATA PANEL

Red-kneed tarantula

Euathlus smithi

Family: Theraphosidae

World population: Unknown

Distribution: Central America and Mexico

Habitat: Scrubland and desert

Size: Length: up to 2.5 in (6.4 cm); leg span: up to 5 in (12.7 cm)

Form: Cephalothorax (arachnid with joined head and thorax); opisthosoma (abdomen) with 4 pairs of strikingly patterned legs; claws for gripping. Eight eyes on head allow all-round (but poor) vision. Males have thin body and long legs; mature males have tibial spurs (sharp projections) on pedipalps (appendages on cephalothorax) to grip female's fangs during mating

Diet: Insects; also small animals such as lizards and mice

Breeding: Female produces up to 700 young a year (often fewer). Eggs wrapped in silk and carried by mother. Spiderlings guarded for several weeks after hatching. Life span of males 7–8 years; females 20–25 years in captivity

Related endangered species: None

Status: IUCN LRnt

The red-kneed tarantula *is strikingly patterned and has been a favorite with collectors.*

Kauai Cave Wolf Spider

Adelocosa anops

The Kauai cave wolf spider is both rare and unusual. Found only in three caves on Kauai Island, Hawaii, the species is blind—unlike other wolf spiders that are known to hunt using their keen eyesight. Endangered from habitat degradation, it is also thought to be at risk from the pesticide residues seeping into its cave dwelling.

Wolf spiders get their name from their habits as hunters. They are swift runners; instead of snaring their victims in silken webs like most other spiders, they rely on speed to chase their prey and run it down, although they may use silk to set up ambushes or "trip wires." They stalk their prey, watching every movement. Once it is trapped, they bite the victim and inject poison through their fang-tipped chelicerae—the first pair of head appendages, which look like miniature elephant tusks when seen through a lens. The venom paralyzes the prey and also digests its tissues, reducing it to a liquid, which the spider can suck out and swallow through its small mouth; they feed particularly on insects such as beetles and ants. There are many species of wolf spider: over 100 in North America and about 50 in Europe. The best-known wolf spider is probably the Mediterranean tarantula. The wolf spider's enemies are wasps, birds, and people. The spiders occur on all continents apart from Antarctica and on many islands, too: Spiders are often among the leading colonizers of volcanic islands.

Wolf spiders are not large and rarely exceed 1 inch (2.5 cm) in length. Their bodies are covered in short hair or bristles, and in the main they are brown or drab in color. As well as the fangs, the head carries a pair of pedipalps (small leglike appendages located in front of the first pair of long walking legs) and (usually) eyes arranged in three rows.

Usually a favorite habitat is leaf litter on forest floors. The spiders excavate shallow burrows and line them with silk spun by the spinnerets on the abdomen. In some species the burrow has a projecting silk entrance tube. The Kauai cave wolf spider, however, is an exception among wolf spiders. It is restricted in its distribution, being found only at three underground locations on the island of Kauai. The caves in which it lives were formed by ancient volcanic lava flows.

Eyes Wide Shut

Although the eyes of most wolf spiders are fairly simple (they have four large and four small eyes), they generally have

DATA PANEL

Kauai cave wolf spider

Adelocosa anops

Family: Lycosidae

World population: Unknown. Surveys of the 3 remaining populations could only find 30 members of each at any one time

Distribution: Kauai Island, Hawaii

Habitat: Dark, moist areas of Kauai cave system, formed from a lava flow and covering about 4 square miles (10 sq. km). About 75% of former habitat has been lost to human activity

Size: Length: 0.5–0.7 in (1.3–1.9 cm); legs: 1 in (2.5 cm)

Form: Head lacks eyes. Reddish-brown carapace (hard, outer covering); pale abdomen and bright-orange legs. Back part of chelicera (pair of fang-tipped appendages on head) has 3 large teeth

Diet: Small, cave-dwelling crustaceans

Breeding: Female lays up to 30 eggs after mating with male. Spiderlings hatch and ride on their mother's back

Related endangered species: Glacier Bay wolf spider (*Pardosa diuturna*) VU; Lake Placid funnel wolf spider (*Sosippus placidus*) VU; rosemary wolf spider (*Lycosa ericeticola*) DD

Status: IUCN EN

Kauai
Oahu
Maui
Hawaii
(UNITED STATES)
Hawaii

Kauai cave wolf spiders *have no eyes (below). More common wolf spiders (right) rely on sight for hunting and courtship rituals. (The male spider on the right is presenting the female with a gift.)*

good eyesight. This is important, since many hunt in poor light conditions. The Kauai cave wolf spider, like many cave-dwelling species, is blind. More unusually, it is eyeless—many cave dwellers cannot see but have vestigial eyes. This makes the species unique. It almost certainly detects the presence of potential prey by touch and smell, and is able to stalk its prey by following their scent trails. Hunting has not been observed, but this species probably feeds primarily on the Kauai cave amphipod, a type of crustacean that is also Endangered. Other species of arthropod that enter the caves from time to time may serve as food for the Kauai cave wolf spider.

Eyesight is usually an important tool in courtship and mating behavior for wolf spiders. How the Kauai cave wolf spider copes is unknown. After mating, the female Kauai cave wolf spider lays eggs—up to 30 at a time. They are laid in a round or oval silk cocoon made by the mother. She fastens it to the tip of her abdomen and carries it everywhere with her until the spiderlings hatch. The young climb onto the mother's back and are carried by her until they are old enough to fend for themselves.

At Risk

As a result of its restricted distribution, the Kauai cave wolf spider is highly endangered. Habitat destruction has occurred through soil filling, quarrying, and other activities associated with development and agriculture. The seepage of pesticide residues into the caves is also thought to be a source of risk. In the delicately balanced environment such problems also affect the Kauai cave amphipod, the spider's main prey. The amphipod feeds on rotting tree roots that work their way into the cave system. If the roots dry out or do not enter the cave, both species are affected.

The Kauai cave wolf spider was added to the IUCN Red List in January 2000. Of the 15 spider species considered to be at risk, six are cave spiders: The tooth cave spider of Texas, for example, was listed as Endangered under the United States Endangered Species Act in 1988. It is the limitation of their habitat that makes wolf spiders especially threatened.

Great Raft Spider

Dolomedes plantarius

Increasing demand for water to sustain expanding populations has made the great raft spider one of Europe's most threatened invertebrate species. Land-reclamation projects have also damaged its habitats by changing the drainage of wetland soils.

The great raft spider is brown or black in color, and strikingly marked with cream or white stripes. It is one of Europe's larger spiders: Its body is nearly 1 inch (2.5 cm) in length, and the span of its furry legs would almost cover the palm of an adult's hand.

The great raft spider is so named because of the way it climbs onto a plant stem and leans over the water to rest its front legs on the surface. By doing this, it is able to detect vibrations generated in the water by prey such as small pondskaters or very small fish. The hairy surface of the spider's body is water repellent, so it does not get wet.

The great raft spider has the characteristic body form of spiders. It is made up of a joined head and thorax (prosoma, or cephalothorax) and abdomen (opisthosoma). The first pair of appendages on the prosoma bears the chelicerae: pincerlike mouthparts or fangs that end in sharp, hollow spikes. They are used to stab prey, subduing it by injecting it with venom.

Wetland Destruction

The main problem for the great raft spider is destruction of its wetland habitat. In the past farmers used to keep the ground fairly clear and in so doing encouraged the growth of smaller plants. The practice was in keeping with the needs of a rural economy. Sedges and reeds, which grew naturally in wetland habitats, were of economic importance and were cut down for use in making thatched roofs. Grass was cut for hay for feeding cattle during the winter.

Below the surface of the soil vegetable matter decomposing in the water formed layers of peat. Peat contains a lot of carbon and is useful for fuel if it is dug out and dried. Digging peat for fuel created many small flooded peat pools that provided habitats for a variety of aquatic plants and animals and hunting grounds for the great raft spider. Keeping the trees under control by cutting them down for brushwood (branches and twigs) for fires also helped keep the ground clear.

Today many of these rural practices have changed. In addition, more wetland is being reclaimed for

---

DATA PANEL

Great raft spider
Dolomedes plantarius

Family: Asauridae

World population: Unknown

Distribution: Northern Europe

Habitat: Wetlands with peat soil

Size: Length (body): up to 1 in (2.5 cm); leg span: up to 3.1 in (8 cm)

Form: Typical spider with 8 legs and 2 main body parts: prosoma, or cephalothorax (joined head and thorax) and pisthosoma (abdomen); 8 eyes; 2 chelicerae (segmented, pincerlike mouthparts) at front of prosoma, ending in fangs connected to venom gland. Spinnarets (fingerlike structures at rear end of opisthosoma) produce silk for webs

Diet: Aquatic insects and very small fish

Breeding: Female lays eggs after mating with male; spiderlings emerge

Related endangered species: No close relatives, but IUCN lists 6 other species in Araneae order as Vulnerable and 6 as Data Deficient, plus the Kauai Cave wolf spider (*Adelocosa anops*) as Endangered

Status: IUCN VU

human use, including the channeling of water to service new developments. The extraction of water for human use from underground aquifers (deposits or rocks such as sandstone containing water) has depleted the supply to the surface. Many of the pools that the spider depended on have also dried up.

Land reclamation projects encourage the growth of more dense vegetation, obliterating the spider's preferred habitat and placing even more pressure on water supplies. However, some of the spider's last refuges have been saved and the damage reversed because commercial water companies need to hold millions of gallons of water in reserve. What was left of the former wetland areas turned out to be suitable

A great raft spider *straddles small pieces of floating vegetation as it rests its front walking legs on the water's surface while trying to detect movements of prey.*

for large-scale water storage. At the same time, the water companies were able to help conserve the great raft spider by protecting its habitat. Such activities, together with the efforts of volunteers, have now had a beneficial effect on great raft spider populations. By removing peat and creating irrigation networks, volunteers have been able to ensure the return of water to the spiders' breeding pools. Water plants such as sedges have become reestablished in the pools, often surviving well on the poor soil.

European Red Wood Ant

Formica polyctena

The European red wood ant brings many benefits to its woodland habitat, aerating the soil with its nest-building activities, and preying on the pests that attack trees. Human encroachment now threatens this fascinating species, and numbers are falling.

European red wood ants are found in wooded areas and on heathland. They excavate underground nests and cover them with a mound of litter from the forest floor, including pine needles, leaf fragments, and twigs.

Every aspect of life in the ant colony is organized for the good of the whole community, and each member has a particular role to play. In *Formica polyctena* there are three castes or classes: workers (sterile females), males, and queens (fertile females). The workers outnumber the other groups in the colony. It is their job to forage for food and building materials outside the nest. They collect the sweet secretions from aphids and prey on other insects, especially small caterpillars. Larger victims are dragged back to the nest by teams of workers. The workers also tend to the queens, look after the grubs and pupae, and defend the colony. The males have only one task: to fertilize the queen's eggs by mating with her. After this they are driven from the nest, and their lives end. The role of the queens is to ensure the reproductive future of the colony and also to found new colonies. This can be done in two ways: either by setting out with a few workers to establish a new colony, or by taking over the colony of a related species such as *Formica fusca*.

When a *fusca* colony is taken over, the *polyctena* queen will displace the resident queen and begin to lay her own eggs in the nest. Remarkably, they will be tended to by the *fusca* workers and reared by them until they become larvae. After a while the *polyctena* workers begin to die out, and a new colony consisting of rufa workers, males, and their queen is in place.

Wood ant colonies need only one or perhaps a couple of queens at any one time. To keep this social balance, the queen secretes hormones and pheromones (chemicals that affect behavior and physiology) that suppress the sexual development of other female ants. The females hatched from the queen's fertilized eggs can therefore only become sterile workers. When the queen dies, the pheromone in the nest decreases, and one or more workers develops into a new queen.

Wood ants do not like to be disturbed and are quick to defend themselves. They squirt formic acid from their abdomens, biting intruders with their powerful jaws, and then attacking the wound with the acid. Few predators are able to withstand this, but the green woodpecker can; it forages in nests to collect the ants with its sticky tongue.

Disturbing the Soil

The wood ant's habitat is seriously at risk from the activities of developers, the timber industry, and timber-related trades. Tree-felling, land drainage, and the mixing of soils by digging and leveling are disturbing areas previously favored by the wood ant. As a result, the number of nests has decreased, and the wood ant is less common today than it was 40 years ago. In addition, agricultural chemicals from nearby fields appear to adversely affect the species or the prey it gathers. At one time the pet shop trade used to raid ant's nests for their pupae to sell as fish food. Fortunately, collection of the mistakenly called "ants' eggs" is now illegal in many parts of Europe because of the damage it causes to colonies.

DATA PANEL

European red wood ant

Formica polyctena

Family: Formicidae

World population: Unknown

Distribution: Europe

Habitat: Woodlands and heaths

Size: Length: queen 0.5 in (1.1 cm); males 0.5 in (1.1 cm); workers 0.4 in (1 cm)

Form: Gray-black abdomen, crossed widthways by black bands; head a deep orange-red color. Both males and queens develop wings at breeding time

Diet: Other insects, especially caterpillars; honeydew from aphids

Breeding: Queen mates once with a male. Her eggs develop into larvae, which then pupate to form cocoons. They hatch into female ants, which become sterile workers. Males are produced when the queen lays unfertilized eggs

Related endangered species: Other species of European red wood ant, including *Formica aquilonia* LRnt and *F. lugubris* LRnt

Status: IUCN LRnt

Worker ants *forage on the woodland floor for food and building materials, turning the soil over and adding to its organic content as they work.*

Hermit Beetle

Osmoderma eremita

Hermit beetles live all their lives in decaying oak and lime trees; successive generations may continue to live in the same tree for many years. Since the beetles do not disperse well, isolated populations build up in each tree; and if the trees fail to survive, the beetles may be lost. The threat of collecting is now further reducing the stability of scarab beetle populations.

Scarab beetles—members of the family Scarabaeidae—display many diverse forms and habits. The family includes dung beetles, the hermit beetle, and the Egyptian sacred scarab beetle. It is thought that the Ancient Egyptians believed that the earth was rotated by a giant scarab beetle in the sky, in the same way that the dung beetle rolls balls of dung. This, at least, is one theory as to why the Egyptians held scarab beetles in such high regard.

Scarab beetles have short legs with flattened middle joints, and a number of species are attractively colored in metallic hues. The head has short antennae and is often equipped with spines or other projections. It is known that the scarab exudes a slightly perfumed scent, but the purpose of it is not understood.

Relatives of scarab beetles include some of the largest beetle species recorded, including the goliath beetle, which is up to 5.8 inches (15 cm) long, and the distinctive tropical rhinoceros beetle, which is about 4 inches (10 cm) long. However, most scarab beetles reach an average length of only 0.6 to 1 inch (1.5 to 2.5 cm).

Rolling Balls

Many members of the family Scarabaeidae are specialized scavengers. Those that forage for dung (animal droppings) are known as dung beetles or "tumblebugs" after the way in which they roll dung balls along the ground and appear to tumble at the same time. (Some beetles just drag the dung pellets along the ground.)

Typical dung beetle behavior involves finding a dung pile, removing a portion of it from the main mass, and rolling this portion into a ball that they roll along the ground. The dung ball is normally much larger than the beetle itself. A beetle measuring about 1 inch (2.5 cm) in length may roll a ball as big as about 4 inches (10 cm) in diameter. It does this while moving backward: It uses its front legs to walk on the ground while its hind legs press on the ball. The task of moving the ball may be shared between individual beetles of the

DATA PANEL

Hermit beetle

Osmoderma eremita

Family: Scarabaeidae

World population: Unknown, decreasing

Distribution: Western, central, and northern Europe

Habitat: Decaying trees: oaks and limes

Size: Length: 1.4 in (3.6 cm), excluding antennae

Form: Beetle with dark-colored body shaped like a narrow shield

Diet: Decaying timber in mature forest

Breeding: Eggs laid in timber develop into grubs (larvae), which metamorphose into adult beetles

Related endangered species: Ciervo scarab beetle (*Aegialia concinna*) VU; Giuliani's dune scarab beetle (*Pseudocotalpa giulianii*) VU

Status: IUCN NT

The hermit beetle *has a body shaped like a shield. It lives in and around hollow, decaying oak and lime trees.*

same species, regardless of their sex. The dung ball is stored in a hole excavated for this purpose, and the beetles return to feed on it. The beetles also store dung in which the females can lay their eggs. The larvae feed inside it, keeping the outer crust intact before emerging as adults.

Dung beetles are found on all continents except Antarctica, and the number of species per continent is roughly in proportion to the number of large mammal species present.

Timber-Loving Beetles

Although related to the dung beetles, the hermit beetle is a timber-loving species that is associated with decaying trees (they particularly like hollow trees). Host trees are usually common oaks or small-leaved lime trees, which are widely distributed across western, central, and northern Europe.

Recent research using radio transmitters suggests that the beetle populations associated with each tree are more or less self-contained, and there is not much exchange of individuals from one tree to the next; for some reason the beetles do not seem to disperse very freely. Consequently, several generations may live continuously in the same tree. This makes them particularly vulnerable if the trees are cut down or the habitat altered in some way.

The hermit beetle larva, or grub, also lives in the decaying wood of the same tree. The grubs of many hermit beetles can generate sounds by rapidly rubbing one part of their bodies against another. The purpose of the sound production, known as stridulation, is unclear. After spending their larval lives feeding on

and developing in the rotting wood, the grubs metamorphose into adult beetles.

Endangered

Areas where oak and lime trees have existed for years are the most likely habitats for hermit beetles, but they are becoming more scarce. Many of the trees favored by hermits have a rich fauna of various other beetle species associated with them, several of which are also threatened.

The hermit beetle is now believed to be endangered across its European distribution. However, it appears to be secure in southern Sweden, where it is being extensively studied. A recent report indicates that the beetles are now being openly traded by collectors using the Internet and other communications vehicles. This represents a further threat to the stability of the the natural populations of hermit beetles.

Blue Ground Beetle

Carabus intricatus

The attractive blue ground beetle is restricted to oak and beech woodlands where there is little undergrowth. Changes in woodland management have caused populations to decline throughout many parts of the beetle's range.

Ground beetles constitute one of the larger families of beetles, with over 40,000 species worldwide. They are common insects outdoors, and occasionally they enter houses and other buildings, but they do not damage household furniture or goods; neither do they pose a threat to people or their pets.

Many beetles have an attractive metallic sheen to their outer surfaces, although black is the most common color. Individual species can normally be identified by the pattern of ornamentations, furrows, grooves, rows of dots, and so on on the outer surfaces of the wing cases. The family includes some very large tropical members, such as the fiddle beetles of Malaysia, whose long, slender head and thorax are combined with the protruding wing cases, imitating the shape of a violin: hence the name.

Ground beetles have a fairly constant shape of an oval, flattened body with medium-length appendages; the shape varies little between the species. The blue ground beetle has a slender body in comparison with other species. The polished wing cases are well developed and in some species are fused together to give additional protection to the underlying wings. The wing cases are formed from the modified first pair of wings, which are not used for flight. The underlying second pair are used for flight in some, but not all, the species. There are many ground beetles that do not fly well and some that do not fly at all.

The head of most ground beetles carries well-developed eyes that are probably important in helping track down their prey, and the antennae (attached to the side of the head) are well developed and prominent. Antennae are also important for hunting, since they are the site of olfaction (smell).

Some species are able to defend themselves by releasing foul-smelling and corrosive liquids. This mechanism serves to ward off quite large predators of the beetle such as toads, birds, and other beetles. The bombardier beetle, for example, sprays a burning cocktail from its tail with an audible cracking noise.

The ground beetles' habit of spending much of their life on the ground or in burrows is reflected in their name. They are active and can move quickly (generally running rather than flying when disturbed). They are predatory and seek out prey by night, sheltering in the daytime under natural cover and hiding under stones, pieces of wood, or other plant debris.

DATA PANEL

Blue ground beetle

Carabus intricatus

Family: Carabidae

World population: Unknown

Distribution: Northwestern and central Europe

Habitat: Temperate woodland dominated by oak and beech trees

Size: Length: adult 0.9–1.4 in (2.4–3.6 cm)

Form: Slender beetle, usually with metallic blue body, but other color variants exist

Diet: Insects, worms, and snails

Breeding: Mating takes place in the fall before winter hibernation. Larvae develop from eggs and feed actively before hiding underground in burrows where they pupate, emerging as adult beetles

Related endangered species: *Carabus olympiae* (no common name) VU; delta green ground beetle (*Elaphrus viridis*) CR

Status: IUCN LRnt

Like the adults, the long, slender ground beetle larvae are carnivorous. They are also active foragers. They do not burrow until it is time for them to pupate into adult beetles.

Because the majority of ground beetles consume insects that are harmful to humans or regarded as pests, they are generally considered beneficial. They eat caterpillars, cockchafer larvae, slugs, and even snails. They have also been introduced as a form of biological control in the United States to keep down the agricultural pest the gypsy moth, which is another introduced species.

Distribution and Habitat

The blue ground beetle has been recorded across much of Europe, from the Mediterranean in the south to Scandinavia in the north, and from Britain in the west to Poland in the east. However, despite its wide overall distribution, it is rare and in decline in most countries, since it is found only in a few localities. It is Britain's largest species of ground beetle and has been recorded there from five sites. However, a survey in 1994 found positive evidence of the species at only two sites there.

The blue ground beetle's preferred habitats are mature woodlands dominated by beech and oak trees where there is little ground vegetation. They like the high humidity provided by the humus layer of the soil, which is derived from rotting leaves and bark. Their narrow range and requirement for a particular set of environmental conditions means that they are regarded as an indicator species for deadwood in Europe. In drought conditions they may become dormant.

Threats to the Species

Habitat change is the main threat to the blue ground beetle. The dense vegetation on the woodland floor is disrupted by changes in grazing patterns or the breaking up of the woodland canopy, which keeps out much of the light. The replacement of deciduous trees by coniferous trees is another threat to the habitat.

There are programs for the restoration of blue ground beetle populations in several European countries. It is hoped that they will allow the reintroduction of laboratory-raised beetles into the wild.

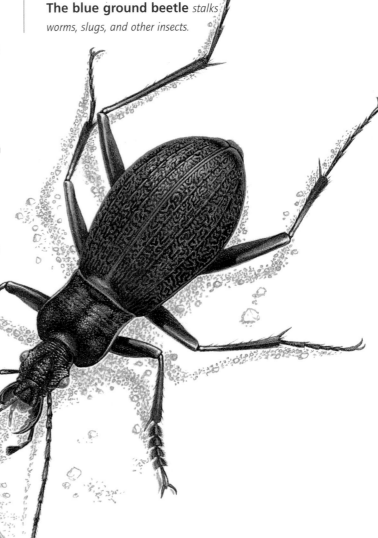

The blue ground beetle *stalks worms, slugs, and other insects.*

Birdwing Butterfly

Ornithoptera alexandrae; O. richmondia

For many years the large, tropical birdwing butterflies have been eagerly sought by collectors, and some birdwings now change hands for substantial sums of money, either legally or illegally. Many are now threatened, and their conservation is hindered by a lack of knowledge of their habits.

Some birdwing butterflies are very large; the Queen Alexandra's birdwing (*Ornithoptera alexandrae*) from Papua New Guinea is, in fact, the largest butterfly in the world, with a wingspan of almost 11 inches (27.5 cm). The Richmond birdwing from Australia, on the other hand, is one of the smaller birdwings, with a wingspan of less than 6 inches (15 cm).

The butterflies' common name is a result of their size and shape; at one time they were said to be shot by hunters who mistook them for birds. As in other *Ornithoptera* species, the sexes differ in color as well as in size: Queen Alexandra males are powder blue, green, gold, and black, and Richmond males are shades of iridescent green and black. The females of both species are dark brown, spotted with white and cream. Female birdwings are generally larger than their male counterparts, although their coloration is less spectacular.

The butterflies have adapted to forest habitats where occasional flowers provide enough nectar to feed the adults. The males exploit certain tall trees as vantage points and as mating sites. Females move around between patches of rain forest in search of specific vines on which to lay their eggs.

Birdwing butterflies have long been favorites with collectors. When all the species were listed by CITES, making it illegal for them to be offered for sale, a lucrative trade in smuggled specimens developed, with single Queen Alexandra's birdwings fetching up to $10,000 for a pair on the black market. Protection from collecting has done little by itself, however, to improve the butterflies' prospects, since the numbers actually changing hands are now small.

Habitat Destruction

A much greater threat comes from the destruction of their habitats and the food plants they live on.

Birdwing caterpillars feed selectively on certain species of tropical forest vine belonging to the genus *Aristolochia*. These vines occur only in rain forest and frequently have a rather patchy distribution, especially where they have suffered from human interference in the form of timber-felling or forest clearing for urban

---

DATA PANEL

Birdwing butterfly: Queen Alexandra's birdwing; Richmond birdwing

Ornithoptera alexandrae; O. richmondia

Family: Papilionidae

World population: Unknown

Distribution: Queen Alexandra's birdwing: Papua New Guinea. Richmond birdwing: subtropical Queensland and New South Wales, Australia

Habitat: Open woodland and tropical rain forest

Size: Wingspan: Queen Alexandra's birdwing: up to 11 in (27.5 cm). Richmond birdwing: less than 6 in (15 cm)

Form: Large butterflies with 2 pairs of conspicuous wings, the leading pair much longer than the second

Diet: Caterpillars feed on forest vine of genus *Aristolochia*; adults on nectar

Breeding: Eggs laid singly on upper side of leaves of host plant; they hatch into caterpillars that feed on plant for about 4 weeks before developing into a chrysalis. Chrysalis hatches into adult butterfly after about 3 weeks

Related endangered species: Obi birdwing butterfly (*Ornithoptera aesacus*) VU; Rothschild's birdwing butterfly (*O. rothschildi*) VU

Status: Queen Alexandra's birdwing IUCN EN. Richmond's birdwing not listed by IUCN

development or farming. Over the past 10 years some important species of the vines have become scarce except in a few national parks, which are not always large enough to guarantee their long-term survival.

The loss of the vines has in turn threatened some of the birdwing species with extinction. The Queen Alexandra's and Richmond birdwings face particularly severe problems. Both have relatively small distributions that are especially vulnerable to forest clearance and the disappearance of food plants and breeding grounds.

Queen Alexandra's birdwing larvae apparently feed exclusively on a particular species of the vine *Aristolochia dielsiana*. Although the vine is widely distributed in Papua New Guinea, it is only available in sufficient quantities to support the huge, ravenous Queen Alexandra's caterpillars in the province of Oro.

Only Oro has enough of the volcanic, phosphate-rich soils that the vines need if they are to flourish. Richmond birdwing larvae depend on another vine, *A. praevenosa*. Their only natural food plant is found in lowland rain forests. However, at higher altitudes—above 2,500 feet (800 m)—on the border ranges of Queensland and New South Wales the Richmond birdwing larvae may also feed on a variant subspecies of *A. deltantha*.

Only when research has figured out all such complexities will biologists fully understand the life cycle of the remarkable birdwing butterflies. Yet such knowledge is necessary if strategies are to be designed to protect them.

Brilliant colors *mark the Richmond birdwing (above) and the Queen Alexandra's birdwing (right), shown here emerging from its chrysalis.*

Apollo Butterfly

Parnassius apollo

Apollo butterflies inhabit areas of difficult terrain and are poorly known. As a result, they have been much sought-after by collectors. There has been a dramatic drop in the number of Apollo butterflies in many areas, and the species is now protected by law in 11 European countries.

The Apollo butterfly is named after Mount Parnassus, a mountain near Delphi in Greece; one of its twin peaks was consecrated to Apollo, the most revered of the Greek gods. According to Greek mythology, Apollo is connected to light and to the sun (Apollo's first name, Phoebus, means bright).

Apollo butterflies are large and are powerful fliers. They may be seen by the fortunate observer during their June to August flight period soaring high above the hillsides, rising and falling with the air currents. Unlike birds, butterflies rarely use soaring flight, so the Apollo is unusual in this respect.

The Apollo butterfly was first described in 1741 by Charles Linnaeus, the Swedish taxonomist, when he was professor of botany at Uppsala University in Sweden. He regarded the species as uncommon in his homeland and thought that it was rarely found elsewhere. It was, in fact, widespread in mountainous areas of Europe. Farther afield, it is known in remote areas of Asia, as far as Mongolia and China.

A number of subspecies are recognized, some of which have been identified only recently. Most species of the butterfly inhabit rocky or mountainous areas above the tree line; they are rarely found in wet areas.

The Apollo is in the same family as the swallowtail butterfly, named after the distinctive "swallow tail" markings on its hind wings. The Apollo is also distinctive. Its red and black markings set against a pale background seem to be a defense against predator birds, which generally do not eat it.

The Apollo's wings are covered with a thin layer of hair, so they can appear translucent. The large size of the wings and their dark markings may help the butterflies absorb warmth from the sun's rays. The furry covering may also help retain heat.

Unusual Caterpillars

Unlike many butterflies, the caterpillar (larva) of the Apollo grows very slowly, taking nearly two years to reach pupation. During its hibernation the caterpillar spins a silk cocoon, which probably serves to protect it from winter frosts. Such behavior is unusual among butterflies.

DATA PANEL

Apollo butterfly

Parnassius apollo

Family: Papilionidae

World population: Unknown

Distribution: Europe; Scandinavia, Alps, and Pyrenees; parts of Asia

Habitat: Mountain ranges at low altitudes

Size: Length: 0.8 in (2 cm); wingspan: 2.8 in (7 cm)

Form: Butterfly with 2 pairs of wings; cream forewings with black markings; hind wings with red markings; body covered in fine scales; wings covered in hair

Diet: Adults eat nectar; caterpillars (larvae) eat alpine vegetation—stonecrops and saxifrages

Breeding: Sexes separate; males mate only once. Egg develops into caterpillar (larva), then chrysalis (pupa), then adult (butterfly)

Related endangered species: *Parnassius autocrator* (no common name) VU; swallowtail butterflies: several species, including Jordan's swallowtail (*Papilio jordani*) VU; cream-banded swallowtail (*P. leucotaenia*) VU

Status: IUCN VU

A related species, *Parnassius autocrator*, has a brilliant orange caterpillar that can release a most unpleasant odor from a gland behind its head. The odor acts as a defense mechanism to warn off predators. The gland, the osmaterium, is present in all Apollo and swallowtail butterfly larvae, but the odor is too faint to be detected by humans.

Sharp Decline

The Apollo has declined rapidly and is considered rare or endangered throughout Europe. It is now protected by law in many European countries.

Among the natural factors that may also be contributing to the decline of Apollo populations are threats from parasites on caterpillars, predators, and competitors for its food. However, many theories for the decline of the Apollo butterfly relate to environmental damage resulting from human activity. They include acid rain caused by pollution, modern agricultural practices, pollution of food plants by traces of heavy metals, overcollecting by enthusiasts, and climate change.

While the exact reasons for the Apollo's decline are still unclear, scientists have discovered that it is quite easy to breed the butterflies. The caterpillars feed on orpine, a species of stonecrop—succulent perennial plants with purplish-white flowers.

Scientific research has assisted in Apollo conservation, and established restoration programs are now underway in several European countries. They include three activities: restoration of former habitats, preparation of suitable new ones, and captive-breeding programs. Researchers are studying the basic conditions needed for successful breeding and population maintenance, especially the climatic requirements of the Apollo butterflies, their preferred grassland habitats, and the abundance and distribution of orpine.

The Apollos, *like the festoons and swallowtails of the same family, are characterized by their bright markings and have the capacity for powerful flight. They are endangered throughout Europe, but breeding programs are enabling numbers to recover.*

Avalon Hairstreak Butterfly

Strymon avalona

The Avalon hairstreak butterfly is named after the town of Avalon on Santa Catalina Island off the coast of southern California. The butterfly is rare, and careful conservation measures are now needed to preserve its habitat and host plants.

Hairstreak butterflies are so called because most species have a fine, light-colored row of dots or hairlike markings running across the underside of both the fore and hind wing, which is visible when the insect is settled with its wings up. The butterflies also have one or more small, taillike extensions on their hind wings.

Hairstreak butterflies are found in Europe, North America, and temperate Asia; the ranges of some North American species extend into South America. Generally, the butterflies do not stray into areas inhabited by people, so they are better seen in woods and open countryside rather than in suburban areas and gardens. Hairstreaks include species with very local distributions.

The butterflies' flight is fast and erratic, and they always settle with the wings closed, thus hiding the coloration of the upper surface. The tails on the hind wings may have an interesting

function in confusing predators. Although those on the Avalon hairstreak are relatively short, in some of its Asiatic relatives they are long and twisted. When the insects settle, the tails are often made to quiver or tremble, and it is thought that some predators mistake them for antennae, thus believing the butterfly is positioned back to front. Attacks on the false antennae tails are less likely to be fatal to the animal than those to the real antennae situated on the head.

The species of hairstreak butterflies that live in temperate regions usually produce one batch of young each year. A few survive the winter as chrysalises or pupae, but the majority do so as eggs, ready to hatch when the weather and plant growth improve. The tropical species reproduce throughout the year, taking only a few weeks to complete their lifecycles.

The caterpillars of many hairstreaks are attended by ants, who "milk" them for honeydew. The ants stroke the caterpillars with their antennae and forelegs. The stimulation encourages the caterpillars

DATA PANEL

Avalon hairstreak butterfly

Strymon avalona

Family: Lycaenidae

World population: Unknown

Distribution: Santa Catalina Island, California

Habitat: Chaparral (dense area of shrubs, brushwood, and trees, especially evergreen oaks, in southwestern U.S.); grassy areas

Size: Wingspan: 0.7–1 in (1.9–2.5 cm)

Form: Typical butterfly. Two pairs of wings; each hind wing bears 1 short "tail." Upper side of wings grayish; upper side of hind wings bear yellow or red spot near the tail and may have small, whitish spots near the edge. Fine, light row of dots or hairline markings on underside of both wings

Diet: Caterpillars feed on silverleaf lotus and deerbrush lotus. Adults feed on nectar from common summac and giant buckwheat

Breeding: Female lays round, flat eggs on terminal and flower bud of silverleaf lotus, island broom, or deerbrush lotus. Sluglike caterpillars (larvae) emerge from February to December

Related endangered species: No close relatives, but 3 other hairstreaks in the U.S. may face similar threats

Status: IUCN VU

to release a sticky, sugary secretion, which the ants eat. In return the ants give the caterpillars protection from small insect predators.

Hairstreak butterflies usually lay eggs that are round and flattened, appearing like minute cookies. With the help of a good lens it is possible to make out geometrical patterns on the eggs. The patterns vary between species. When the caterpillars emerge, they look rather sluglike in shape. They feed on the flowers and leaves of trees and bushes rather than on herbaceous plants.

In the case of the Avalon hairstreak butterfly, which is one of the rarest and most isolated butterfly species in the United States, the female lays her eggs at the end of the stems and on the flower buds of the silverleaf lotus plant. The lotus has silvery-green leaves and clusters of orange flowers. The female also lays eggs on the island broom or deerbrush lotus, with its rich, green foliage and clusters of yellow and orange flowers. Hatching takes place between February and December, when broods of caterpillars emerge from the eggs to feed on the plants. Toward the end of the hatching period adults may also be seen. The adults feed on nectar from the bunches of small, cream-white flowers of the laurel or common sumac. They also take nectar from the flowers of the giant buckwheat or St. Catharine's lace. St. Catharine's lace is only found on Santa Catalina.

The Avalon hairstreak *has a row of fine, pale hairline markings on the underside of its wings and thin, taillike extensions on the hind wings.*

Isolated Existence

The Avalon hairstreak is endemic to Santa Catalina Island, which means it is found nowhere else. The isolated position of the island has allowed the butterfly to survive free from pressures such as predators or competition by species with similar requirements. Such pressures may have led to the butterfly's extinction on the mainland. It is possible, however, that the Avalon hairstreak may have evolved on Santa Catalina Island.

The need for conservation of the Avalon hairstreak is appreciated by the authorities, who have done much to publicize its vulnerability.

Hermes Copper Butterfly

Lycaena hermes

The Hermes copper is an endangered butterfly with a distribution limited to the district around San Diego and the adjacent northern end of Baja California. It is especially susceptible to habitat damage by developers and fire.

California is home to a great number of butterfly species. Over 100 have been recorded from Orange County alone. The wide range of habitats found in the state, from barren open or wooded mountains through cool river gorges to hot coastal plains and offshore islands, means that there have been many opportunities for new species to evolve in specialized habitats. In some cases the habitats are fragile and are now subject to pressures from development; in others the areas are small (like some offshore islands) and so are also vulnerable.

The California Department of Fish and Game is concerned for the future of many species of butterfly that are listed as rare or endangered within the state. Their concerns are shared by the United States Fish and Wildlife Service, especially where the future of breeding rests on many small, separate populations.

One such species is the Hermes copper, a member of the family Lycaenidae (gossamer-winged butterflies). The family is represented by about 100 species in North America and has four groups: the coppers, the blues, the hairstreaks, and the harvesters. A relative of the highly restricted and endangered Avalon hairstreak butterfly, the Hermes copper occurs around San Diego and at the northern end of Baja California. Although not striking in appearance, the Hermes copper has one spikelike tail on each of its hind wings, giving it a slightly swallowtail appearance. It can be confused with hairstreak butterflies, so its wing markings are important in identification.

Like many Californian butterflies, the Hermes copper relies on a specialized habitat with particular plants and climate, so its geographical distribution is local and patchy. It inhabits woodlands, preferably where there is a good mix of tree species, chaparral (dense growth of shrubs and trees), and coastal sage scrub. Such habitats provide the necessary plant hosts, including the redberry of the buckthorn family, for caterpillars to feed on. The butterflies have survived close to suburban San Diego as a result of the buckthorn's distribution. The adults feed on nectar from the flowers of wild buckwheat.

DATA PANEL

Hermes copper butterfly

Lycaena hermes

Family: Lycaenidae

World population: Unknown

Distribution: California; range restricted to San Diego County and adjacent Baja California

Habitat: Mixed woodlands, chaparral (dense growth of shrubs and trees), and coastal scrub

Size: Wingspan: 1–1.3 in (2.5–3.2 cm)

Form: Typical butterfly; 2 pairs of conspicuous wings; each hind wing bears 1 short "tail." Upper side brown with yellow-orange patch surrounding black spots; underside bright yellow; forewing with 4–6 black spots; hind wing with 3–6 black spots. Caterpillars (larvae) are apple to dark green and have much simpler eyes than adult butterflies

Diet: Caterpillars feed on redberry. Adults feed on nectar from flowers of wild buckwheat

Breeding: Male settles on plants to watch for females. Single eggs are laid on twigs of caterpillar host plant, redberry; pupae hatch from end of May to mid-June. After hatching, the young caterpillars feed on the new young shoots of host plant

Related endangered species: Avalon hairstreak butterfly (*Strymon avalona*) VU

Status: IUCN VU

UNITED STATES

MEXICO

Hermes copper butterflies have good eyesight, which is important in the mating behavior. They have a pair of typical insect compound "eyes" on the head consisting of many individual visual units (known as omatidia). Moving and static objects can be viewed accurately. The markings on the butterfly's wings are important in the recognition of members of the same species and the initiation of mating behavior. Male butterflies perch on twigs looking out for females to mate with. Eggs are laid singly on the twigs of the host plant and do not hatch until the following spring. At this time of year the young leaf buds on the host plant are shooting and able to provide the necessary food for the caterpillars.

Habitat Hazards

Increasing urban growth is causing a serious problem for wildlife in California and other rapidly developing parts of the United States. The construction of domestic and industrial building sites, new roads, and electricity lines causes fragmentation—the breaking up of habitats into smaller and smaller sectors. The fragmented areas become separated by man-made barriers, and wild animals are not able to move around as freely as they once could. As a result, individual breeding groups become isolated from each other. Some wild species, including insects such as butterflies, become restricted to remnants of habitat that are no longer big enough to support them. This reduces the overall breeding strength of the population.

Another major problem for butterfly colonies is forest fires. Fires start easily in the dry climate, and the butterflies, along with their food plants, are constantly at risk. The continued widespread use of pesticides

Hermes copper butterflies *in flight and at rest, displaying the species' distinctive wing markings.*

and herbicides is also damaging to adult butterflies, their caterpillars, and their food plants.

The Hermes copper is listed locally as rare or local throughout its range, and a strategy is needed to protect it from further habitat loss and fragmentation. An increase in public awareness, particularly among local government officers and within the construction industry, would greatly help its future.

Giant Clam

Tridacna gigas

The strange, massive, and beautiful giant clam has fueled the imaginations of storywriters, though its reputation for closing its giant shells around the limbs of unfortunate explorers is unfounded. Easily collected by souvenir hunters, large giant clams are now rare.

The giant clam, which belongs to the phylum Mollusca, is distinctive for its size and bright color. The animals are giants among invertebrates, showing the basic bivalve mollusk body plan, but on a huge scale. Giant clams are found in tropical seas, where they live in shallow water among reef-building corals. Two massive, thick valves (shells) are hinged together to protect the soft body. In living specimens the gape of the shells reveals bright and often vividly colored flesh.

Giant clams are generally sedentary, living attached to rocks and corals with the hinge downward and the free open edges of the valves upward. Smaller individual clams attach to the substratum by a byssus (a mass of strong threads that are secreted by the clam). Using grinding movements of the shell, they burrow slightly so as to nestle into the rocky reef surface. Large specimens are heavy enough not to need attachment.

Slow-Growing Giants

Giant clams are very slow growing: The thick shells are gently secreted as calcium carbonate by the outer skin, or mantle, of the clam. This exposed part of the mantle tissue contains iridescent colors created by colorless crystalline solid purine. The crystals act like minute lenses; they concentrate any perceptible light that penetrates the water on the myriad microscopic plants that live in the mantle tissue in a symbiotic relationship with the clam. The plants, known as zooxanthellae, make sugars and proteins, and ultimately form part of the giant clam's food supply. Eventually, the photosynthetic products (those created using sunlight as an energy source) find their way into the clam's energy budget. In return the clam supplies them with carbon dioxide for photosynthesis and the nitrogen and minerals they need to make proteins.

Giant clams are filter feeders, and the other element of the clam's food comes from microscopic plankton that are drawn into the body via the inhaling siphon and the gills. The gills are covered with cells bearing beating cilia (fine threadlike extensions) that drive the water across them and serve to sort and select suitable food particles that are then directed to the gastric tract. The gills are also responsible for gas exchange; while collecting food, the clams take up oxygen and release carbon dioxide. The exhaust water stream leaves via the exhaling siphon. Both siphon openings can be seen when the clam shells gape.

Easy Targets

Unlike many other bivalves, the adults are virtually immobile, so they are easy game for souvenir hunters. Their shells have been used in native societies as house decorations and even as baptismal fonts! They have also been exploited since the 1960s to supply the Taiwanese market's demand for giant clam adductor muscle for human consumption. In 1983 the International Union for the Conservation of Nature (IUCN) identified severe depletion of the species, particularly in the coral reefs of Indonesia, the Philippines, Papua New Guinea, Micronesia, and southern Japan. Fortunately, techniques for cultivating the giant clam were developed during the late 1980s. They are now cultivated in hatcheries in the Asia-Pacific region and used to restock depleted reefs.

DATA PANEL

Giant clam

Tridacna gigas

Family: Tridacnidae

World population: Unknown

Distribution: Asia-Pacific regions

Habitat: Attached to rocks and corals in shallow water

Size: Length across: may reach 41 in (104 cm). Weight: up to 500 lb (227 kg)

Form: Typical bivalve shell shape with scalloped shells; colored mantle visible at gape

Diet: Minute drifting planktonic organisms and the products of photosynthesis by zooxanthellae (microscopic plants) that live in the mantle

Breeding: Each is hermaphroditic; a free-swimming planula larva results from external fertilization of eggs. It attaches itself to a new substrate and develops into a new colony, which produces new zooids (independent animal bodies)

Related endangered species: Probably many, including red coral (*Corallium rubrum*), which is exploited in the Mediterranean Sea

Status: IUCN VU

The giant clam *has thick shells with corrugated edges. It is an imposing resident of shallow sea margins.*

California Bay Pea Crab

Parapinnixa affinis

Pea crabs are tiny crabs, almost always less than half an inch (1 cm) wide. As adults they live associated with other marine animals such as bivalve mollusks (clams) and tubeworms.

The California Bay pea crab inhabits the tubes and burrows of polychaete worms (marine annelid worms of the class Polychaeta that bear bristles and have paired appendages). Other species of pea crab, such as *Pinnotheres pisum*, are found in mussel and cockle shells in European coastal waters, while females of *Pinnotheres ostreum*, also known as the oyster crab, are found in oysters of the Atlantic coastal waters of North America and are abundant in oysters of Chesapeake Bay. (The males are usually free-swimming.)

Pea crabs live in other animal hosts but do not derive nourishment from their hosts' tissues; animals with this arrangement are not parasites but are known as commensal indwellers. The pea crabs appear to do no serious physical harm or damage to their hosts, although they do not seem to do any particular good either.

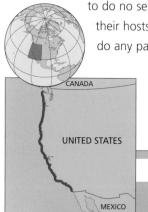

Unlike other crabs, which are protected by a hard exoskeleton made from calcium carbonate, pea crabs have a soft body. They rely on their hosts to provide them with shelter and protection.

The pea crabs intercept some of the food sieved from the water by the gills of the host animal. They feed on small prey items such as planktonic animals and carrion scraps that find their way near to or into the host's tube or shell.

Pea crabs sometimes live in pairs, although the male may move around between hosts. The female will carry the fertilized eggs under her abdomen until they hatch. At this point a planktonic larva swims away from the tube or burrow and goes through several stages, feeding on other planktonic organisms until it is sufficiently developed to settle on the seabed and seek out a new invertebrate host.

A study of the morphology (form and structure) of animals can tell us a lot about their lifestyles and adaptations to their favorite habitats. The strange shape of the California Bay pea crab, being much wider than it is long, is a perfect adaptation to life in a tube: It can move up and down its home by walking sideways, particularly aided by the well-developed next

DATA PANEL

California Bay pea crab

Parapinnixa affinis

Family: Pinnotheridae

World population: Unknown

Distribution: Western seaboard of U.S., especially coast of California

Habitat: The tubes and burrows of marine polychaete worms, including *Terebella californica* and *Amphitrite* species

Size: Minute crabs, reaching about 0.1 in (2.5 mm) long and 0.2 in (5 mm) wide

Form: Minute, wide crabs with very well-developed 4th pair of walking legs quite out of proportion to the rest of their body

Diet: Small marine animals and carrion

Breeding: Male fertilizes eggs that are carried on female's abdomen. Here they are guarded, oxygenated, and protected until they hatch into free-swimming planktonic larvae. They

pass through several stages, feeding on plankton before they metamorphose, settle on the seabed, and seek out a new suitable host worm

Related endangered species: None

Status: IUCN EN

The California Bay pea crab *(left) is less than 0.20 in (5 mm) wide— about a quarter of the size of the tiny California fiddler crab (below), which is distinguished by its large claw (in the male), used to signal to mates. The fiddler crab lives in burrows in sandy mud in bays and estuaries from Southern California to Baja California. Its future is also uncertain as a result of encroachment on its habitat by human construction.*

to last pair of walking legs. Pea crabs of the species *Pinnotheres pisum* have much more rounded bodies, reflecting the fact that they do not live in such confined spaces.

The relative softness of the California Bay pea crab's shell contributes to its overall flexibility and helps when it moves around in confined spaces. In some pea crab species there is a marked difference in the shape of the claws in the males and females, which probably assists the male in holding the female during mating.

Vulnerability

The viability of pea crabs depends on the availability of hosts as well as the presence of other essentials such as food and reproductive mates. Many of the worm species that the California Bay pea crab relies on are subjected to population fluctuations. These events in turn affect the population of the pea crabs that live with them.

Records of animals as small as pea crabs are often lacking, so it is difficult to establish a broad view of their distribution and abundance. The California Bay pea crab is listed as Endangered by the IUCN, and the extent of threats to the animal will be resolved only as a result of more scientific research.

Horseshoe Crab

Limulus polyphemus

Despite their name, horseshoe crabs are not crustaceans like other crabs, lobsters, and shrimps. They are related to scorpions, spiders, and the extinct trilobites.

Horseshoe crabs, or king crabs, are among the strangest-looking marine invertebrates. They belong to a class of their own called Merostomata. Different species occur in two distinct parts of the world: the eastern seaboard of North America and in Southeast Asia, which suggests that they are the last surviving representatives of an ancient group that was once widely distributed in the world's oceans. Fossil horseshoe crabs have been found in rocks in Germany dating back to Jurassic times, and the crabs are sometimes referred to as living fossils.

The dominant feature of the crabs is a domed carapace (hard shield), which carries a pair of compound eyes (made up of many separate visual units) at its side and a smaller pair of simple eyes nearer the midline. Behind the domed carapace is a triangular abdomen that bears a pointed tail spine, or telson.

Turning the carapace over reveals that its leading edge is clearly horseshoe shaped; hence the name. There are six pairs of jointed legs, an arrangement that suggests the crab's affinity with spiders and scorpions. The first legs include a pair of small feeding appendages ending in nippers (corresponding to the chelicerae, or fang-bearing appendages of a spider's head); there are five more pairs of appendages, the first of which corresponds to the pedipalps, or leglike sensory limbs of the spider's head. The last pair of appendages bears additional spines to help the crab get a grip on the sand. Just above the "knee joint" there are swollen, toughened extensions called gnathobases that can press together and are used for crushing prey and preparing it for swallowing. Such tools are essential because much of the crab's prey—such as clams and snails—has shells. Under the abdomen are a series of flaplike structures that assist with swimming and fast movement over the sand. They pump water over the respiratory surface of the gill "books"—thin plates well supplied with blood vessels and arranged a bit like the pages in a book. The tail spine stabilizes the crab as it moves around on the sand.

As in many marine animals, reproduction in the horseshoe crab is controlled by the

DATA PANEL

Horseshoe crab

Limulus polyphemus

Family: Limulidae

World population: Unknown

Distribution: Coastal waters of India, Indonesia, Malaysia, Philippines, Singapore, Thailand, Taiwan, and Vietnam; Atlantic coasts of Canada, U.S., and Mexico

Habitat: Sandy or muddy shores and shallow water in bays and estuaries

Size: Length: up to 60 cm. Weight: adults 0.7–1 oz (20–30 g)

Form: Fossillike, armored invertebrate with conspicuous tail. Six pairs of jointed appendages, including pair of feeding appendages ending in nippers

Diet: Small bivalves, worms, and other invertebrates; occasionally seaweed

Breeding: Males clasp tail of female and are towed around by her. Female digs shallow pit on midshore and lays 200–300 eggs; male sheds sperm over them. Larvae, known as trilobite larvae because they resemble the fossil trilobites, emerge. Several larval stages are marked by molts. Maturity is reached after 16 molts and at about 10 years

Related endangered species: Three other marine invertebrates that share the common name horseshoe crab: *Carcinoscorpius rotundicauda* DD, *Tachypleus gigas* DD, and *T. tridentatus* DD

Status: IUCN LRnt

moon and tides. Breeding takes place in spring and summer. At full moon, when the highest tides occur, females move up the beach to lay their eggs. A male clings onto each female and is dragged up the beach. The female digs a shallow pit just above the high-tide mark and lays her eggs in it. The male fertilizes the eggs as they are laid. Then they are covered with sand and left alone.

Cause for Concern

The future of the horseshoe crab is a cause for concern among conservationists. For many years the animals were regarded as a common sight on the shore and in the shallow water of their native seas.

Horseshoe crabs *congregate at the edge of the tide. They can swim on their backs using their gill flaps, but they also plow through sand or mud, arching their bodies and pushing with the tail spine and last pair of legs.*

When they come ashore to breed, the animals become vulnerable to disturbance by people.

Like other bottom-dwelling marine arthropods, horseshoe crabs are easily caught. In Asia they are collected for food by local people. However, while they have been used in the souvenir trade, it is their collection for industrial use, such as for making chicken food and fertilizers, that seems to have most seriously affected horseshoe crab populations.

Cushion Star

Asterina phylactica

The cushion star was not identified as a separate species until 1979. Previously it had been classified with the gibbous starlet, a slightly larger starfish that lacks the conspicuous darker star pattern found on the upper surface of the cushion star.

Cushion stars are starfish (sea stars) with five thick, short arms. Starfish are themselves not fish, but echnoderms: spiny-skinned marine invertebrates of the class Asteroidea, and they are different from most other types of animal. Their bodies are star-shaped with (usually five) rays, or arms, surrounding an indistinct disk. They have no brain and no obvious eyes or other conspicuous sense organs. The lack of eyes and other sensory equipment does not mean that they cannot detect stimuli such as touch, chemicals, or light. In fact, the outer surface of a starfish plays an important role in detecting predators and food. The body is covered with spines and microscopic grooming organs that resemble minute forceps or tongs.

The mouth is situated on the underside of the body; the intestine rises up through the center of the animal with a digestive pocket branching out into each of the five rays.

Under the starfish's rays are grooves with rows of feet tipped by suckers that help them grip rocks and manipulate prey. Most species of starfish feed on small animals such as worms and crustaceans. The prey are either manipulated whole into the mouth using the tube feet or eaten—remarkably—by extending the stomach out through the mouth, wrapping it around the victim, and digesting it outside the starfish body.

Scientists did not recognize the cushion star as a distinct species of starfish until 1979. Before then it was classified with the gibbous starlet *Asterina gibbosa* because of its similar size and appearance. The cushion star is slightly smaller and has a conspicuous darker star pattern on its upper surface.

Crucial Stages of Growth

Typically, starfish are dioecious (sexes are separate). Some, however, are hermaphrodites (having both male and female reproductive organs) and pass through a male phase before becoming females. Some species brood (sit on, or hatch) their eggs in a process that is similar to the the brooding of birds, except that no heat is transferred; others release the eggs into the water where they are fertilized externally.

Both the cushion star and gibbous starlet are hermaphrodites, and both lay eggs attached to the rocks. However, while the gibbous starlet abandons its eggs after they have been laid, the cushion star stays with its eggs and broods them.

DATA PANEL

Cushion star

Asterina phylactica

Family: Echinidae

World population: Unknown

Distribution: Mediterranean Sea and northeastern Atlantic

Habitat: Rock pools and shallow water down to 66 ft (20 m)

Size: Up to 0.6 in (1.5 cm) across

Form: Typical starfish form with 5 short rays (arms); body surface covered with short spines. On underside grooves contain rows of tube feet tipped with suckers

Diet: Small animals such as worms and crustaceans

Breeding: Adults are hermaphrodites (having both male and female organs). Eggs are laid on rocks and brooded by parent until they metamorphose into juveniles

Related endangered species: None

Status: Not listed by IUCN; not listed by CITES

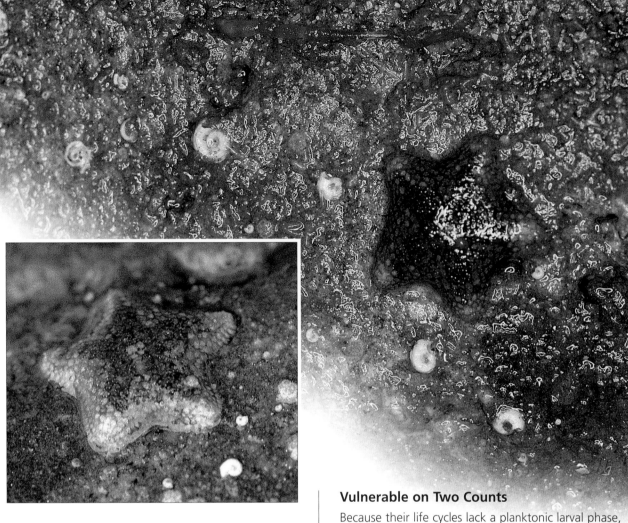

The cushion star *on a rocky shore; suckers on the feet help it cling to the rock. Respiration takes place through structures in the skin.*

Unusually, there is no larval phase in the cushion star and gibbous starlet. In the majority of starfish fertilized eggs develop into larvae, which join the community of plankton—floating plants and animals that are suspended in the surface waters and move by means of the currents rather than by active swimming. (Plankton means "drifting" in Greek.) There they feed on minute planktonic plants before metamorphosis occurs. The larval stage allows the distribution of the species around the world's seas, avoids competition with the adults for food and living space in one area, and ensures a healthy mixing of genetic material.

Vulnerable on Two Counts

Because their life cycles lack a planktonic larval phase, the gibbous starlet and cushion star cannot disperse their young widely. As a result, the adult populations are not well mixed genetically and are therefore more vulnerable as a species. According to the extent of their geographical isolation, they may evolve into different races or even into new species.

The cushion star has not yet been placed on the IUCN Red Data List, but it is a suitable candidate. Its distribution in northwestern Europe and the Mediterranean Sea is local and patchy.

Evidence shows that the cushion star is vulnerable to oil pollution. An oil spillage in Wales in 1996 seriously reduced the population because it depends on clean rocks to brood its young after the eggs have been laid. Then, when the oil killed off the adults, there were no planktonic larvae to recolonize the area.

Freshwater Mussel

Margaritifera auricularia

About 10 species of freshwater mussels occur in Europe, and more are found in America. Generally they are inconspicuous members of the lake and riverbed animal communities, but two—in the genus Margaritifera—have become famous for their pearls, and overcollection has endangered them.

Freshwater mussels are bivalve mollusks: Their bodies are enclosed within two shells that are attached by a hinge. They have many structural features in common with their marine relatives the common mussel and the common oyster. The shells, technically known as valves, are secreted by the outer skin of the body that is called the mantle. The mantle and the shells cover the whole body and also enclose a space referred to as the mantle cavity. The shells and mantle cavity open along the underside of the animal as well as at the front and back.

Inside a Mussel Shell

Many of the important daily activities of the mussel—such as respiration, feeding, excretion, reproduction, and even activities related to locomotion—take place inside the mantle space. When the mussel is in its normal orientation, the hinge of the shells is on the upper side. Immediately below the hinge area, inside the shells, lies the main body. It includes the

head, mouth, digestive tract, digestive organs, reproductive organs, and heart. Hanging down into the mantle cavity are two pairs of gills, one on the left side and one on the right. They run the whole length of the shells. Between each pair, in the middle, is a hydraulically operated foot, which is extended by blood pressure. The head is poorly developed in relation to the rest of the body, and it lacks complex receptor organs like eyes, but it has a pair of leaflike palps that have a sensory function and assist in the ingestion of food.

The shells can be closed tightly together by the contraction a pair of adductor muscles that run from one shell to the other. When the muscles contract and close the shells, they also compress a rubbery ligament, which is sandwiched between them near the hinge. The adductor muscles have special qualities that enable them to contract for long periods of time. When the muscles relax, the compressed, rubbery ligament forces the shells open like a spring.

Freshwater mussels mainly inhabit muds, sands, and gravels on the beds of rivers and lakes. They

DATA PANEL

Freshwater mussel (Spengler's freshwater mussel)

Margaritifera auricularia

Family: Margaritiferidae

World population: Unknown, declining

Distribution: Europe, from Portugal east to the Czech Republic

Habitat: Freshwater rivers, streams, and lakes through which rivers flow

Size: Length: up to 5 in (12 cm)

Form: Typical mussel or clam shape; body enclosed in 2 shells

Diet: Plant plankton and detrital particles

Breeding: Larvae develop from fertilized eggs carried internally on the mussel's gills and are expelled when they have developed hooks;

they catch hold of the fins of passing fish and get carried around for about 2 weeks before they drop off and complete their development on the river or lake bed

Related endangered species: Freshwater pearl mussel (Margaritifera margaritifera) EN; Louisiana pearlshell (M. hembeli) CR; Alabama pearlshell (M. marrianae) EN

Status: IUCN CR

normally live with part of their bodies buried, and they achieve this using the foot. The foot is inflated with blood and extends down between the shells into the substratum. Its tip then widens and forms an anchor in the sediment. By using the foot, the freshwater mussel can stay in the substratum or move itself slowly along, plowing through the sediment with a jerky movement.

The gills are major organs that are also found inside the mantle cavity. They are made up of vertically arranged filaments covered in fine, beating threads called cilia that are invisible to the naked eye. The beating cilia create a current so that water is drawn in at the rear between the shells and passed across the surface of the gills. Here oxygen is absorbed into the body from the water, and carbon dioxide is passed out into the water. As is so often the case in the animal kingdom, a ciliated respiratory stream of water is also used for feeding, and the gills serve a second function as sieves to strain suitable particles of food from the water currents.

Freshwater mussels *are able to anchor themselves to a river or lake bed by means of a hydraulically operated foot. The foot also allows jerky movement through the sediment.*

Overcollection for Pearls

Bivalve mollusks like oysters and mussels are well known for the way in which they respond to irritants from foreign bodies or parasites inside the shell. A coating of nacre, the pearly innermost layer of the bivalve shell, is deposited around the intrusion, and as it is secreted, a pearl grows. *Margaritifera auricularia* and its close relative *Margaritifera margaritifera* are known for their ability to form pearls, which although being less lustrous than the traditional oyster pearls, are still desirable. Overcollection of freshwater mussels in search of pearls has caused a serious reduction in their populations. In fact, numbers of *Margaritifera auricularia* have been so depleted that the IUCN has classified the species as Critically Endangered.

Starlet Sea Anemone

Nematostella vectensis

The starlet sea anemone was not discovered until 1929. Its small size and burrowing lifestyle make the animal difficult to study. The same factors also make an assessment of the threats to its survival problematic.

The starlet anemone was first discovered in the mud at the bottom of a rock pool at Bembridge on the Isle of Wight, off the south coast of England, in 1929. The first scientific description of it did not appear until 1935.

The starlet is one of the least known and smallest of the 1,000 or more species of sea anemone. It measures just 0.3 to 0.7 inches (1 to 2 cm) long. It is difficult to make out much of its structural detail without the aid of a low-powered microscope.

Most small, aquatic creatures are very sensitive to the amount of salt present in water—the salinity. However, a feature of the starlet sea anemone is its ability to tolerate a wide range of salinities, from about 9 parts salt per thousand parts water to 37.7 parts salt per thousand parts water. (Normal coastal seawater is about 34 parts salt per thousand parts water.) The starlet anemone therefore thrives in environments such as lagoons and salt marshes in which salinity fluctuates. It favors coastal lagoons where fine mud overlies gravel or shingle. It has also been found in brackish creeks and pools in salt marshes.

Unlike many sea anemones, the starlet lacks a structure called an adhesive basal disk, which allows it to attach itself to rocks and shell. Instead, it has a burrowing organ called a physa that enables it to burrow into mud from where it can remain hidden and protected in wait for its prey. The physa does, however, have small adherent spots, called rugae, that stick to surfaces such as pebbles and pieces of vegetation so that the animal can exist without sediment in to which to burrow. Because they become attached to pieces of algae or seaweed, starlet sea anemones are collected inadvertently.

Patient Predator

Like all sea anemones, the starlet is an opportunistic, sit-and-wait predator. Its oral disk (mouth) is surrounded by two rings of transparent tentacles: an outer ring of six long, trailing tentacles and an inner ring of seven shorter, upstanding ones. The tentacles

DATA PANEL

Starlet sea anemone
(Isle of Wight anemone)

Nematostella vectensis

Family: Edwardsiidae

World population: Unknown

Distribution: Coastal lagoons in northwestern Europe and the U.S.

Habitat: Brackish (slightly salty) lagoons; ponds in salt marshes

Size: Length: 0.3–0.7 in (1–2 cm)

Form: Cylindrical, transparent body; twin circles of tentacles surrounding mouth; hollow tentacles. The transparent, jellylike substance that makes up most of body, as in a jellyfish, is called mesogloea

Diet: Animal plankton (minute, drifting animals)

Breeding: Unknown

Related endangered species: Ivell's sea anemone (*Edwardsia ivelli*) DD

Status: IUCN VU

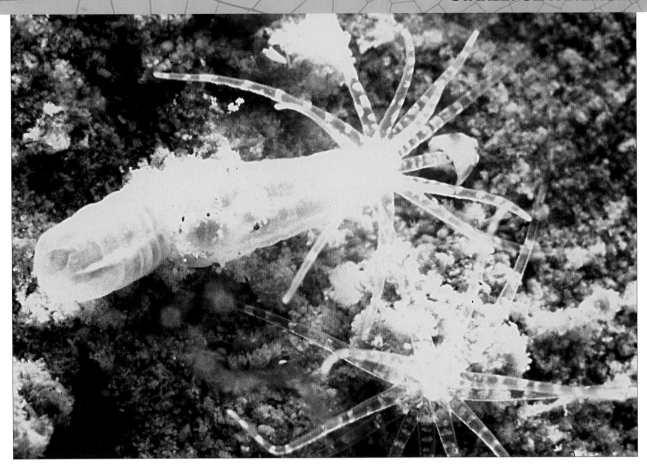

are armed with stinging cells that can immobilize and subdue animal plankton (tiny animals that drift at the water's surface) that collide with them.

Threats to Survival

Small, burrowing species such as the starlet sea anemone are difficult to find and even more difficult to study and assess in terms of their vulnerability and conservation status. There are probably many thousands of small, short-lived invertebrates, as yet undiscovered, whose precise status would be equally difficult to establish. A relative of the starlet anemone, for example, Ivell's sea anemone, was discovered in a brackish lagoon in Sussex on the south coast of England. The two species are very similar in appearance, but the distribution of Ivell's sea anemone appears to be extremely limited. Recent attempts to relocate the animal have failed, raising the question of whether Ivell's sea anemone has become extinct.

The starlet sea anemone *is less than an inch long. Like other sea anemones, it has a hollow, cylindrical body (polyp) with a ring of tentacles around the mouth.*

The main threat to the starlet sea anemone is urban development and human activities along the coast. Its brackish lagoon habitat is under pressure both from developers and from changes to drainage and sediment accumulation caused by human populations. The dumping of rubbish in the vicinity of lagoons is also a threat, since it can result in an increase in nitrogen levels in the water. This can cause a rapid growth surge in aquatic algae—an algal bloom. Algal blooms cause adverse physical and chemical changes in the water; they can result in the depletion of nutrients available to other species and release poisons into the environment. Such factors could be a threat not only to the starlet sea anemone but also to other as yet undiscovered species.

EX

EW

CR

EN

VU

NT

LC

O

Partula Snails

Partula spp.

Snail species of the genus Partula *inhabit islands in the Pacific Ocean. In the absence of natural predators they have become well-adapted to their conditions. However, the snails have been unable to cope with predator snails introduced by people (ironically, to curb the effects of other snail pests). A rescue plan has now helped ensure the Partula snail's survival.*

Many people are familiar with the story of the Galápagos Islands in the Pacific Ocean; each of the islands in the remote archipelago (island group) has its own characteristic animal life adapted to the individual conditions. On other islands of the South Pacific a similar situation exists, this time for small, relatively inconspicuous snails of the genus *Partula*. The environmental conditions on each island are slightly different, and in the absence of most natural predators such as amphibians, reptiles, and mammals the snails have evolved to become well adapted to the conditions on their island. With the passage of time distinct species of *Partula* became established on the different islands. However, the snails were not adapted to cope with the changes to their habitat brought about by the activities of people.

Specialist Snails

Snails and slugs are gastropods, the largest group in the phylum Mollusca. They live in freshwater or marine habitats or on the ground. Terrestrial snails and slugs have evolved to breathe air and feed mostly on land plants. They are so successful as herbivores that they often come to our attention as agricultural or garden pests. Unlike other plant eaters, snails can release enzymes into their gut that are capable of digesting the cellulose in the cell walls of plants. Other herbivores, such as rabbits, cows, and sheep, have to use microscopic organisms to do this, and their intestines have adapted places to accommodate the microorganisms. *Partula* snails are terrestrial. They rely for their food on the rotting stems of hibiscus plants. Such a specialized diet makes them more vulnerable to threats than some other species.

DATA PANEL

Partula snail

***Partula* spp.**

Family: Partulacea

World population: Varies according to species; less than 50 Polynesian tree snails (*P. affinis*)

Distribution: Islands of French Polynesia, Micronesia, and South Pacific Ocean

Habitat: Trees of natural rain forest

Size: Length: up to 1.2 in (3 cm)

Form: Small but typical snail. Most species have pointed shell; a few have rounded shells; 2 pairs of retractile tentacles, the rear pair bearing eyes

Diet: Rotting vegetation

Breeding: Hermaphrodites (both male and female sex organs are present) and livebearers: give birth to single, shelled young measuring 0.1 in (3 mm)

Related endangered species: About 15 species of *Partula* are extinct

Status: Seventy-nine *Partula* species are listed by the IUCN. Many are classified as Extinct, while some (for example, Polynesian tree snail, *P. affinis*) are classed as Critically Endangered

Partula tohiveana (left) from French Polynesia is classified by the IUCN as Extinct in the Wild. Shell forms and patterns differ between species, and much can be learned about previous generations from dead snails.

this time the carnivore Englandia rosea, was brought to the islands to prey on it. However, instead of attacking the giant snails, it turned its attention on the native Partula snails. The results were devastating for the native snails, who were no match for the predators. In just 10 years many Partula snails were extinct.

A conservation program led by the London Zoo in Britain has done much to ensure the survival of some Partula snails in the region. By collecting some of the surviving snails and taking them back to London Zoo, the scientists have been able to raise snails in captivity. Now many of the snails bred in the zoo have been reintroduced to their native islands. Special reserves have been created where the snails can reestablish themselves free from competition and predators, and more are being planned.

Partula snails are also slow breeding; each adult snail usually produces only one snail at a time. As a result, population growth can never be rapid, and this fact makes them vulnerable to increases in pressure from predators.

Introduced Predators

In the 1960s the giant African land snail was brought to some of the islands by farmers and bred to provide food. Immigrant snails escaped from the snail farms and quickly established themselves in the wild. Soon these populations were out of control. With no natural predators existing on the islands, the snail became a pest, devouring crops and other valuable plants.

In order to bring the giant African land snails under control, a second species of immigrant snail,

A Success Story

Island habitats, with their limited but often unique local diversity, are ideal nurseries for new specialized species. However, as the story of the Partula snail shows, it can be dangerous to introduce foreign species, even those brought in for biological pest control. Zoos regularly make contributions to conservation programs, and relatively humble animals like snails can benefit from their expertise as much as the endangered birds and mammals that just catch the public imagination.

Categories of Threat

The status categories that appear in the data panel for each species throughout this book are based on those published by the International Union for the Conservation of Nature (IUCN). They provide a useful guide to the current status of the species in the wild, and governments throughout the world use them when assessing conservation priorities and in policy-making. However, they do not provide automatic legal protection for the species.

Animals are placed in the appropriate category after scientific research. More species are being added all the time, and animals can be moved from one category to another as their circumstances change.

Extinct (EX)

A group of animals is classified as EX when there is no reasonable doubt that the last individual has died.

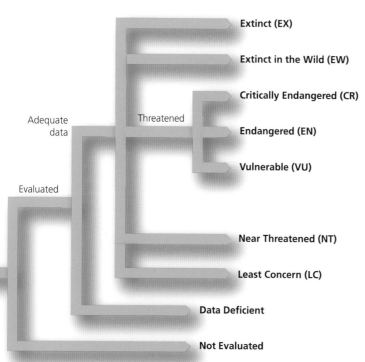

- Extinct (EX)
- Extinct in the Wild (EW)
- Critically Endangered (CR)
- Endangered (EN)
- Vulnerable (VU)
- Near Threatened (NT)
- Least Concern (LC)
- Data Deficient
- Not Evaluated

Threatened

Adequate data

Evaluated

Extinct in the Wild (EW)

Animals in this category are known to survive only in captivity or as a population established artificially by introduction somewhere well outside its former range. A species is categorized as EW when exhaustive surveys throughout the areas where it used to occur consistently fail to record a single individual. It is important that such searches be carried out over all of the available habitat and during a season or time of day when the animals should be present.

Critically Endangered (CR)

The category CR includes animals facing an extremely high risk of extinction in the wild in the immediate future. It includes any of the following:

- Any species with fewer than 50 individuals, even if the population is stable.
- Any species with fewer than 250 individuals if the population is declining, badly fragmented, or all in one vulnerable group.
- Animals from larger populations that have declined by 80 percent within 10 years (or are predicted to do so) or three generations, whichever is the longer.

The IUCN categories *of threat. The system displayed has operated for new and reviewed assessments since January 2001.*

• Species living in a very small area—defined as under 39 square miles (100 sq. km).

Endangered (EN)

A species is EN when it is not CR but is nevertheless facing a very high risk of extinction in the wild in the near future. It includes any of the following:

• A species with fewer than 250 individuals remaining, even if the population is stable.

• Any species with fewer than 2,500 individuals if the population is declining, badly fragmented, or all in one vulnerable subpopulation.

• A species whose population is known or expected to decline by 50 percent within 10 years or three generations, whichever is the longer.

• A species whose range is under 1,900 square miles (5,000 sq. km), and whose range, numbers, or population levels are declining, fragmented, or fluctuating wildly.

• Species for which there is a more than 20 percent likelihood of extinction in the next 20 years or five generations, whichever is the longer.

Vulnerable (VU)

A species is VU when it is not CR or EN but is facing a high risk of extinction in the wild in the medium-term future. It includes any of the following:

• A species with fewer than 1,000 mature individuals remaining, even if the population is stable.

• Any species with fewer than 10,000 individuals if the population is declining, badly fragmented, or all in one vulnerable subpopulation.

• A species whose population is known, believed, or expected to decline by 20 percent within 10 years

The capture and *export of red-kneed tarantulas for the pet trade is banned in Mexico, but some smugglers continue to act illegally.*

or three generations, whichever is the longer.
• A species whose range is less than 772 square miles (20,000 sq. km), and whose range, numbers, or population structure are declining, fragmented, or fluctuating wildly.
• Species for which there is a more than 10 percent likelihood of extinction in the next 100 years.

Near Threatened/Least Concern (since 2001)

In January 2001 the classification of lower-risk species was changed. Near Threatened (NT) and Least Concern (LC) were introduced as separate categories. They replaced the previous Lower Risk (LR) category with its subdivisions of Conservation Dependent (LRcd), Near Threatened (LRnt), and Least Concern (LRlc). From January 2001 all new assessments and reassessments must adopt NT or LC if relevant. But the older categories still apply to many animals until they are reassessed, and will also be found in this book.
• Near Threatened (NT)
Animals that do not qualify for CR, EN, or VU categories now but are close to qualifying or are likely to qualify for a threatened category in the future.
• Least Concern (LC)
Animals that have been evaluated and do not qualify for CR, EN, VU, or NT categories.

Lower Risk (before 2001)

• Conservation Dependent (LRcd)
Animals whose survival depends on an existing conservation program
• Near Threatened (LRnt)

Animals for which there is no conservation program but that are close to qualifying for VU category.

By monitoring *populations of threatened animals like this American rosy boa, biologists help keep the IUCN Red List up to date.*

Pollution-free *ponds and lakes are crucial for the survival of orange-spotted emeralds and other dragonflies.*

• Least Concern (LRlc)
Species that are not conservation dependent or near threatened.

Data Deficient (DD)

A species or population is DD when there is not enough information on abundance and distribution to assess the risk of extinction. In some cases, when the species is thought to live only in a small area, or a considerable period of time has passed since the species was last recorded, it may be placed in a threatened category as a precaution.

Not Evaluated (NE)

Such animals have not yet been assessed.

Note: a colored panel in each entry in this book indicates the current level of threat to the species. The two new categories (NT and LC) and two of the earlier Lower Risk categories (LRcd and LRnt) are included within the band LR; the old LRlc is included along with Data Deficient (DD) and Not Evaluated (NE) under "Other," abbreviated to "O."

CITES *lists animals in the major groups in three Appendices, depending on the level of threat posed by international trade.*

	Appendix I	Appendix II	Appendix III
Mammals	277 species 16 subspecies 14 populations	295 species 12 subspecies 12 populations	45 species 8 subspecies
Birds	152 species 11 subspecies 2 populations	1,268 species 6 subspecies 1 population	35 species
Reptiles	75 species 5 subspecies 6 populations	527 species 4 subspecies 4 populations	55 species
Amphibians	16 species	98 species	
Fish	15 species	71 species	
Invertebrates	62 species 4 subspecies	2,100 species 1 subspecies	17 species

CITES APPENDICES

Appendix I lists the most endangered of traded species, namely those that are threatened with extinction and will be harmed by continued trade. These species are usually protected in their native countries and can only be imported or exported with a special permit. Permits are required to cover the whole transaction—both exporter and importer must prove that there is a compelling scientific justification for moving the animal from one country to another. This includes transferring animals between zoos for breeding purposes. Permits are only issued when it can be proved that the animal was legally acquired and that the remaining population will not be harmed by the loss.

Appendix II includes species that are not currently threatened with extinction, but that could easily become so if trade is not carefully controlled. Some common animals are listed here if they resemble endangered species so closely that criminals could try to sell the rare species pretending they were a similar common one. Permits are required to export such animals, with requirements similar to those Appendix I species.

Appendix III species are those that are at risk or protected in at least one country. Other nations may be allowed to trade in animals or products, but they may need to prove that they come from safe populations.

CITES designations are not always the same for every country. In some cases individual countries can apply for special permission to trade in a listed species. For example, they might have a safe population of an animal that is very rare elsewhere. Some African countries periodically apply for permission to export large quantities of elephant tusks that have been in storage for years, or that are the product of a legal cull of elephants. This is controversial because it creates an opportunity for criminals to dispose of black market ivory by passing it off as coming from one of those countries where elephant products are allowed to be exported. If you look up the African elephant, you will see that it is listed as CITES I, II, and III, depending on the country location of the different populations.

Organizations

The human race is undoubtedly nature's worst enemy, but we can also help limit the damage caused by the rapid increase in our numbers and activities. There have always been people eager to protect the world's beautiful places and to preserve its most special animals, but it is only quite recently that the conservation message has begun to have a real effect on everyday life, government policy, industry, and agriculture.

Early conservationists were concerned with preserving nature for the benefit of people. They acted with an instinctive sense of what was good for nature and people, arguing for the preservation of wilderness and animals in the same way as others argued for the conservation of historic buildings or gardens. The study of ecology and environmental science did not really take off until the mid-20th century, and it took a long time for the true scale of our effect in the natural world to become apparent. Today the conservation of wildlife is based on far greater scientific understanding, but the situation has become much more complex and urgent in the face of human development.

By the mid-20th century extinction was becoming an immediate threat. Animals such as the passenger pigeon, quagga, and thylacine had disappeared despite last-minute attempts to save them. More and more species were discovered to be at risk, and species-focused conservation groups began to appear. In the early days there was little that any of these organizations could do but campaign against direct killing. Later they became a kind of conservation emergency service—rushing to the aid of seriously threatened animals in an attempt to save the species. But as time went on, broader environmental issues began to receive the urgent attention they needed. Research showed time and time again that saving species almost always comes down to addressing the

Conservation *organizations range from government departments in charge of national parks, such as Yellowstone National Park (right), the oldest in the United States, to local initiatives set up to protect endangered birds. Here (above) a man in Peru climbs a tree to check on the nest of a harpy eagle discovered near his village.*

problem of habitat loss. The world is short of space, and ensuring that there is enough for all the species is very difficult.

Conservation is not just about animals and plants, nor even the protection of whole ecological systems. Conservation issues are so broad that they touch almost every aspect of our lives, and successful measures often depend on the expertise of biologists, ecologists, economists, diplomats, lawyers, social scientists, and businesspeople. Conservation is all about cooperation and teamwork. Often it is also about helping people benefit from taking care of their wildlife. The organizations involved vary from small groups of a few dozen enthusiasts in local communities to vast, multinational operations.

THE IUCN

With so much activity based in different countries, it is important to have a worldwide overview, some way of coordinating what goes on in different parts of the planet. That is the role of the International Union for the Conservation of Nature (IUCN), also referred to as the World Conservation Union. It began life as the International Union for the Preservation of Nature in 1948, becoming the IUCN in 1956. It is relatively new compared to the Sierra Club, Flora and Fauna International, and the Royal Society for the Protection of Birds. It was remarkable in that its founder members included governments, government agencies, and nongovernmental organizations. In the

years following the appalling destruction of World War II, the IUCN was born out of a desire to draw a line under the horrors of the past and to act together to safeguard the future.

The mission of the IUCN is to influence, encourage, and assist societies throughout the world to conserve the diversity of nature and natural systems. It seeks to ensure that the use of natural resources is fair and ecologically sustainable. Based in Switzerland, the IUCN has over 1,000 permanent staff and the help of 11,000 volunteer experts from about 180 countries. The work of the IUCN is split into six commissions, which deal with protected areas, policy-making, ecosystem management, education, environmental law, and species survival. The Species Survival Commission (SSC) has almost 7,000 members, all experts in the study of plants and animals. Within the SSC there are Specialist Groups concerned with the conservation of different types of animals, from cats to flamingos, deer, ducks, bats, and crocodiles. Some particularly well-studied animals, such as the African elephant and the polar bear, have their own specialist groups.

Perhaps the best-known role of the IUCN SSC is in the production of the Red Data Books, or Red Lists. First published in 1966, the books were designed to be easily updated, with details of each species on a different page that could be removed and replaced as new information came to light.

By 2010 the Red Lists include information on about 45,000 types of animal, of which almost 10,000 are threatened with extinction. Gathering this amount of information together is a

The IUCN Red Lists *of threatened species are published online and can be accessed at:*
http://www.
iucnredlist.org

huge task, but it provides an invaluable conservation resource. The Red Lists are continually updated and are now available on the World Wide Web. The Red Lists are the basis for the categories of threat used in this book.

CITES

CITES is the Convention on International Trade in Endangered Species of Wild Fauna and Flora (also known as the Washington Convention, since it first came into force after an international meeting in Washington D.C. in 1973). Currently 175 nations have agreed to implement the CITES regulations. Exceptions to the convention include Iraq and North Korea, which, for the time being at least, have few trading links with the rest of the world. Trading in animals and their body parts has been a major factor in the decline of some of the world's rarest species. The IUCN categories draw attention to the status of rare species, but they do not confer any legal protection. That is done through national laws.

Conventions serve as international laws. In the case of CITES, lists (called Appendices) are agreed on internationally and reviewed every few years. The Appendices list the species that are threatened by international trade. Animals are assigned to Appendix I when all trade is forbidden. Any specimens of these species, alive or dead (or skins, feathers, etc.), will be confiscated by customs at international borders, seaports, or airports. Appendix ll species can be traded internationally, but only under strict controls. Wildlife trade is often valuable in the rural economy, and this raises difficult questions about the relative importance of animals and people. Nevertheless, traders who ignore CITES rules risk heavy fines or imprisonment. Some rare species—even those with the highest IUCN categories (many bats and frogs, for example)—may have no CITES protection simply because they have no commercial value. Trade is then not really a threat.

The Greenpeace ship, *seen here in Antarctica, travels to areas of conservation concern and helps draw worldwide media attention to environmental issues.*

WILDLIFE CONSERVATION ORGANIZATIONS

BirdLife International
BirdLife International is a partnership of 60 organizations working in more than 100 countries. Most partners are national nongovernmental conservation groups such as the Canadian Nature Federation. Others include large bird charities such as the Royal Society for the Protection of Birds in Britain. By working together within BirdLife International, even small organizations can be effective globally as well as on a local scale. BirdLife International is a member of the IUCN.
Web site: http://www.birdlife.org

Conservation International (CI)
Founded in 1987, Conservation International works closely with the IUCN and has a similar multinational approach. CI offers help in the world's most threatened biodiversity hot spots.
Web site: http://conservation.org

Durrell Wildlife Conservation Trust (DWCT)
Another IUCN member, the Durrell Wildlife Conservation Trust was founded by the British naturalist and author Gerald Durrell in 1963. The trust is based at Durrell's world-famous zoo on Jersey in the Channel Islands. Jersey was the world's first zoo dedicated solely to the conservation of endangered species. Breeding programs at the zoo have helped stabilize populations of some of the world's most endangered animals. The trust trains conservationists from many countries and works to secure areas of natural habitat to which animals can be returned. Jersey Zoo and the DWCT were instrumental in saving numerous species from extinction, including the pink pigeon, Mauritius kestrel, Waldrapp ibis, St. Lucia parrot, and the Telfair's skink and other reptiles.
Web site: http://durrell.org

Fauna & Flora International (FFI)
Founded in 1903, this organization has had various name changes. It began life as a society for protecting large mammals, but has broadened its scope. It was involved in saving the Arabian oryx from extinction.
Web site: http://www.fauna-flora.org

National Audubon Society
John James Audubon was an American naturalist and wildlife artist who died in 1851, 35 years before the society that bears his name was founded. The first Audubon Society was established by George Bird Grinnell in protest against the appalling overkill of birds for meat, feathers, and sport. By the end of the 19th century there were Audubon Societies in 15 states, and they later became part of the National Audubon Society, which funds scientific research programs, publishes

WILDLIFE CONSERVATION ORGANIZATIONS

magazines and journals, manages wildlife sanctuaries, and advises state and federal governments on conservation issues. Web site: http://www.audubon.org

Pressure Groups

Friends of the Earth, founded in Britain in 1969, and Greenpeace, founded in 1971 in British Columbia, were the first environmental pressure groups to become internationally recognized. Greenpeace became known for "direct, nonviolent actions," which drew attention to major conservation issues. (For example, campaigners steered boats between the harpoon guns of whalers and their prey.)

The organizations offer advice to governments and corporations, and help those that seek to protect the environment, while continuing to name, shame, and campaign against those who do not.

Royal Society for the Protection of Birds

This organization was founded in the 1890s to campaign against the slaughter of birds to supply feathers for the fashion trade. It now has a wider role and has become Britain's premier wildlife conservation organization, with over a million members. It is involved in international activities, particularly in the protection of birds that migrate to Britain. Web site: http://www.rspb.org.uk

The Sierra Club

The Sierra Club was started in 1892 by John Muir and is still going strong. Muir, a Scotsman by birth, is often thought of as the founder of the conservation movement, especially in the United States, where he campaigned for the preservation of wilderness. It was through his efforts that the first national parks, including Yosemite,

Sequoia, and Mount Rainier, were established. Today the Sierra Club remains dedicated to the preservation of wild places for the benefit of wildlife and the enjoyment of people. Web site: http://www.sierraclub.org

World Wide Fund for Nature (WWF)

The World Wide Fund for Nature, formerly the World Wildlife Fund, was born in 1961. It was a joint venture between the IUCN, several existing conservation organizations, and a number of successful businesspeople. Unlike many charities, WWF was big, well-funded, and high profile from the beginning. Its familiar giant panda emblem ranks alongside those of the Red Cross, Mercedes Benz, or Coca-Cola in terms of instant international recognition. Web site: http://www.wwf.org

GLOSSARY

adaptation Features of an animal that adjust it to its environment; may be produced by evolution—e.g., camouflage coloration

adaptive radiation Where a group of closely related animals (e.g., members of a family) have evolved differences from each other so that they can survive in different niches

adult A fully grown sexually mature animal

amphibious Able to live on both land and in water

amphipod A type of crustacean found on land and in both fresh and seawater

annelid Of the phylum Annelida in which the body is made up of similar segments, e.g., earthworms, lugworms, and leeches

anterior The front part of an animal

arachnid One of a group of arthropods of the class Arachnida, characterized by simple eyes and four pairs of legs. Includes spiders and scorpions

Aristotle's lantern Complex chewing apparatus of sea-urchins that includes five teeth

arthropod The largest phylum in the animal kingdom in terms of the number of species in it. Characterized by a hard, jointed exoskeleton and paired jointed legs. Includes insects, spiders, crabs, etc.

biodiversity The variety of species and the variation within them

biome A major world landscape characterized by having similar plants and animals living in it, e.g., desert, rain forest, forest

canopy Continuous (closed) or broken (open) layer in forests produced by the intermingling of branches of trees

carrion Rotting flesh of dead animals

cephalothorax A body region of crustaceans formed by the union of the head and thorax. See prosoma

chelicerae The first pair of appendages ("limbs") on the prosoma of spiders, scorpions, etc. Often equipped to inject venom

chrysalis The pupa in moths and butterflies

cocoon The protective coat of many insect larvae before they develop into pupae or the silken covering secreted to protect the eggs

crustacean Member of a class within the phylum Arthropoda typified by five pairs of legs, two pairs of antennae, a joined head and thorax, and calcerous deposits in the exoskeleton; e.g., crabs, shrimps, etc.

deforestation The process of cutting down and removing trees for timber or to create open space for growing crops, grazing animals, etc.

diatoms Microscopic single-celled algae

DNA (deoxyribonucleic acid) The substance that makes up the main part of the chromosomes of all living things; contains the genetic code that is handed down from generation to generation

dormancy A state in which—as a result of hormone action—growth is suspended and metabolic activity is reduced to a minimum

dorsal Relating to the back or spinal part of the body; usually the upper surface

ecology The study of plants and animals in relation to one another and to their surroundings

ecosystem A whole system in which plants, animals, and their environment interact

ectotherm Animal that relies on external heat sources to raise body temperature; also known as "cold-blooded"

epitoke A form of marine annelid having particularly well developed swimming appendages

exoskeleton A skeleton covering the outside of the body or situated in the skin, as found in some invertebrates

extinction Process of dying out at the end of which the very last individual dies, and the species is lost forever

gene The basic unit of heredity, enabling one generation to pass on characteristics to its offspring

hermaphrodite An animal having both male and female reproductive organs

incubation The act of keeping the egg or eggs warm or the period from the laying of eggs to hatching

indwellers Organisms that live inside others, e.g., the California Bay pea crab, which lives in the tubes of some marine annelid worms, but do not act as parasites

indigenous Living naturally in a region; native (i.e., not an introduced species)

insect Any air-breathing arthropod of the class Insecta, having a body divided into head, thorax, and abdomen, three pairs of legs, and sometimes two pairs of wings

invertebrates Animals that have no backbone (or other bones) inside their body, e.g., mollusks, insects, jellyfish, crabs

krill Planktonic shrimps

larva An immature form of an animal that develops into an adult form through metamorphosis

mantle cavity A space in the body of mollusks that contains the breathing organs

metamorphosis The transformation of a larva into an adult

nematocyst The stinging part of animals such as jellyfish, usually found on the tentacles

ocelli Markings on an animal's body that resemble eyes. Also, the tiny, simple eyes of some insects, spiders, crustaceans, mollusks, etc.

parasite An animal or plant that lives on or within the body of another (the host) from which it obtains nourishment. The host is often harmed by the association

pedipalps Small, paired leglike appendages immediately in front of the first pair of walking legs of spiders and other arachnids. Used by males for transferring sperm to the females

plankton Animals and plants drifting in open water; many are minute

polyp Individual organism that lives as part of a colony—e.g., a coral—with a saclike body opening only by the mouth that is usually surrounded by a ring of tentacles

posterior The hind end or behind another structure

prosoma The joined head and thorax of a spider, scorpion, or horseshoe crab

pupa An insect in the stage of metamorphosis between a caterpillar (larva) and an adult (imago)

spawning The laying and fertilizing of eggs by fish and amphibians and some mollusks

test An external covering or "shell" of an invertebrate such as a sea-urchin; it is in fact an internal skeleton just below the skin

thorax (thoracic, adj.) In an insect the middle region of the body between the head and the abdomen. It bears the wings and three pairs of walking legs

ventral Of or relating to the front part or belly of an animal (see dorsal)

wing case One of the protective structures formed from the first pair of nonfunctional wings, which are used to protect the second pair of functional wings in insects such as beetles

Books

Insects

Eaton, Eric R. and Kaufman, Kenn. *Kaufman Field Guide to Insects of North America*, Houghton Mifflin, New York, U.S., 2007

Pyle, Robert Michael, National Audubon Society *Field Guide to North American Butterflies*, Pyle, Robert Michael, A. Knopf, New York, U.S., 1995

Mammals

Macdonald, David, *The New Encyclopedia of Mammals,* Oxford University Press, Oxford, U.K., 2009

Payne, Roger, *Among Whales*, Bantam Press, U.S., 1996

Reeves, R. R., and Leatherwood, S., *The Sierra Club Handbook of Whales and Dolphins of the World*, Sierra Club, U.S., 1983

Sherrow, Victoria, and Cohen, Sandee, *Endangered Mammals of North America*, Twenty-First Century Books, U.S., 1995

Whitaker, J. O., Audubon Society *Field Guide to North American Mammals,* Alfred A. Knopf, New York, U.S., 1996

Wilson, Don E., Mittermeier, Russell A., *Handbook of Mammals of the World Vol 1,* Lynx Edicions, Barcelona, Spain, 2009

Birds

Attenborough, David, *The Life of Birds,* BBC Books, London, U.K., 1998

BirdLife International, *Threatened Birds of the World*, Lynx Edicions, Barcelona, Spain and BirdLife International, Cambridge, U.K., 2000

del Hoyo, J., Elliott, A., and Sargatal, J., eds., *Handbook of Birds of the World Vols 1 to 15,* Lynx Edicions, Barcelona, Spain, 1992–2010

Dunn, Jon, and Alderfer, Jonathan K., *National Geographic Field Guide to the Birds of North America,* National Geographic Society, Washington D.C., United States, 2006.

Stattersfield, A., Crosby, M., Long, A., and Wege, D., eds., *Endemic Bird Areas of the World: Priorities for Biodiversity Conservation,* BirdLife International, Cambridge, U.K., 1998

Fish

Buttfield, Helen, *The Secret Lives of Fishes*, Abrams, U.S., 2000

Dawes, John, and Campbell, Andrew, eds., *The New Encyclopedia of Aquatic Life, Facts On File*, New York, U.S., 2004

Reptiles and Amphibians

Corbett, Keith, *Conservation of European Reptiles and Amphibians,* Christopher Helm, London, U.K., 1989

Corton, Misty, *Leopard and Other South African Tortoises,* Carapace Press, London, U.K., 2000

Hofrichter, Robert, *Amphibians: The World of Frogs, Toads, Salamanders, and Newts*, Firefly Books, Canada, 2000

Murphy, J. B., Adler, K., and Collins, J. T. (eds.), *Captive Management and Conservation of Reptiles and Amphibians*, Society for the Study of Amphibians and Reptiles, Ithaca, New York, 1994

Stafford, Peter, *Snakes*, Natural History Museum, London, U.K., 2000

General

Allaby, Michael, *A Dictionary of Ecology*, Oxford University Press, New York, U.S., 2010

Douglas, Dougal, and others, *Atlas of Life on Earth*, Barnes & Noble, New York, U.S., 2001

Web sites

http://www.nature.nps.gov/ U.S. National Park Service wildlife site

http://www.ummz.lsa.umich-edu/ umich.edu/ University of Michigan Museum of Zoology animal diversity web. Search for pictures and information about animals by class, family, and common name

http://www.cites.org/ CITES and IUCN listings. Search for animals by order, family, genus, species, or common name. Location by country and explanation of reasons for listings

http://www.cmc-ocean.org Facts, figures, and quizzes about marine life

www.darwinfoundation.org/ Charles Darwin Research Center

http://www.fws.gov.endangered Information about endangered animals and plants from the U.S. Fish and Wildlife Service, the organization in charge of 94 million acres of wildlife refuges

http://www.endangeredspecie.com Information, links, books, and publications about rare and endangered species. Also includes information about conservation efforts and organizations

*http://*www.ewt.org.za Endangered South African wildlife

http://forests.org/ Includes forest conservation answers to queries

http://www.iucn.org Details of species, IUCN listings, and IUCN publications. Link to online Red Lists of threatened species at: www.iucnredlist.org

http://www.pbs.org/journeytoamazonia The Amazonian rain forest and its unrivaled biodiversity

http://www.ucmp.berkeley.edu/echinodermata The echinoderm phylum—starfish, sea-urchins, etc.

INDEX

Words and page numbers in **bold type** indicate main references to the various topics.